# GOING ON TO SALVATION
# A Study in the Wesleyan Tradition

*Maxie D. Dunnam*

*A study guide for the Christian pilgrimage of
"faith working through love," as envisioned by
John Wesley and practiced by the people called Methodist.*

DISCIPLESHIP RESOURCES
MATERIALS FOR GROWTH IN CHRISTIAN FAITH AND LIFE
P.O. Box 189 • Nashville, TN 37202 • Phone (615) 340-7284

ISBN 0-88177-100-7

Library of Congress Catalog Card Number: 90-62269

DR100B

# Contents

# Dedication

TO
The Reverend David H. McKeithen who brought
me into the Methodist fold and guided my first
stumbling steps in the ministry;

TO
The congregation of Christ United Methodist
Church, Memphis, Tennessee, who call forth the
best that is in me as preacher, allow me the joy of
being their pastor, and support me with their prayers
and mutual ministry—to whom the basic content of
this book was preached to launch our celebration of
the Bicentennial Year of Methodism in America;

AND TO
Methodist congregations I have served in McLain,
Beaumont, Leaf, Avant, Gautier, and Gulfport,
Mississippi; Atlanta, Georgia; San Clemente and
Anaheim, California. "I thank my God upon every
remembrance of you."

# *Foreword*

This book serves a dual purpose. It can and should be read, along with the Bible and *The Upper Room,* as devotional literature, for it is charged with inspiration, and there is the heartbeat of passion and zeal in every paragraph. It was written, however, to instruct the reader in fundamental Wesleyan doctrine. This the author does in a clear, direct, and convincing style comparable to Wesley's own manner of writing. The theme of the book is apparent from beginning to end. The author does not detour from his purpose or run off into side issues which preclude the accomplishment of his task.

The book lays bare Wesley's concept of salvation. All the doctrines are in place and are properly arranged, so that, in reading, one moves logically, step by step, from the desperate plight of sin, in which all are involved, through forgiveness and regeneration, to holiness and a life well pleasing to God.

The author admits that his concern is not with Christianity in general but rather with Methodism in particular. Therefore, he delineates the unique doctrinal features of Wesley's thought and, above all else, the Wesleyan spirit.

This book is much more than an essay in historical theology. It is an explication of the relevance of Wesley's thought today and an invitation to reflect and to share this relevance in one's own experience. The book is done almost in picture language, so that one sees as one reads and the impressions made on one's mind are indelible. The illustrations used are gripping and powerful, and even those out of the past are contemporary because they are timeless.

The author, Maxie Dunnam, is one of the most prominent and effective preachers in the English-speaking world. His writings, especially in devotional literature, have become minor classics. This book can but add to his stature and renown.

WILLIAM R. CANNON
A Bishop of The United Methodist Church and
Honorary President of the World Methodist Council

# Introduction

I'm a United Methodist by choice, though I have a great legacy of Christian experience from other traditions. My grandfather, Lewis Dunnam, was a Freewill Baptist preacher—the closest to a "circuit rider" we have in our family. He "walked" his circuit. I grew up in Southern and Missionary Baptist churches, but experienced throughout my childhood and early adolescence the brush arbor revivals of independent evangelists and the itinerant preachers who more often than not preached on the front porches of homes as folks stood around in the yard.

I was converted in a little Southern Baptist church in rural Mississippi and baptized at the hands of Brother Grissom in a rather cold creek in early September. My mother and father are active in that church today—my father, a deacon.

I knew only one Catholic before I went to college. He was a normal sort of fellow, but we thought it strange that he and his family would drive thirty miles each Sunday to get to a Catholic church for mass. Interestingly, during the past fifteen years, Roman Catholic writers have been primary sources of spiritual nurture for me; and one of the most meaningful relationships I have is with the Ecumenical Institute of Spirituality—twenty-five persons, among whom are eight Roman Catholics, along with Quakers, Orthodox, Episcopalians, Lutherans, Presbyterians, and others.

I became a Methodist by choice about three years after my conversion. Doctrine had a lot to do with it—style also. But I wouldn't diminish the influence of a Methodist preacher, David McKeithen, a warm, loving human being who cared deeply for people, took time with a teenage boy, and preached the gospel thoughtfully and with deep conviction. I began to feel the call to preach, and I felt that should I ever answer that call, I ought to be in the "right" church for me. I began to read and talk to people, and eventually made the choice, surprising David and his congregation when I walked down the aisle on a Sunday morning to offer myself as a member. Then a year later, I offered myself to that same congregation as a "candidate for ministry" (though we didn't call it that then).

So, I'm a United Methodist by choice, and it thrilled me when Chester Custer, then executive director of Discipleship Resources, invited me to write this book.

As I began this work, a cartoon came to my attention. It pictured a pastor in a very large pulpit. His head was withdrawn deep into his shoulders as if he were trying to escape something. His mouth was turned downward; his eyes looked blank. He was truly forlorn; he was a pitiful sight. There was a layman beside the pulpit obviously trying to help him, but what he was doing was unusual. On a nearby stool, there was a large battery. The clips of a jumper cable had been attached to the terminals. The layman had a clip in each hand, and he was reaching toward the pastor. The top of the pastor's head had been swung open, and the layman was reaching in with the jumper cable.

In the foreground of the cartoon was the front row of the congregation. A smiling lady was leaning over to speak to some folks who were obviously visitors. She said very matter-of-factly, "Sometimes the pastor needs a little help getting started."

Funny as it is, it's true. It's hard to get started—not just on a sermon but on a book like this. How do you begin to talk about the Christian journey as the Wesleys and early Methodists saw it? In a volume this size, decisions of emphasis have to be made, and some things we hold firmly have to be left out. This is tough, but essential.

I'm not going to deal specifically with that which we hold in common with all orthodox Christians, such as our belief in the Trinity, in God, in Jesus Christ, in the Holy Spirit, the Bible, the Resurrection, etc. Rather, I want to deal with the way of salvation as understood and experienced in the Wesleyan movement. That doesn't mean that what I say about a particular theme will be unique to United Methodism; it simply means that I'm going to put together in these chapters that which, as I understand it, is the heartbeat, the distinct content, and to some degree the style of who we are as United Methodists—particularly as viewed by John Wesley.

The reason it's so hard for me to get started is that I am basically an impatient person. I have problems pacing myself; therefore, my temptation is to want to say it all. I don't want to leave out anything. Also, I have this almost neurotic passion to speak freshly, and at the same time, clearly. So I find myself wrestling with the dilemma of expressing a 2000-year-old gospel, and our 250-year-old expression of that gospel in a fresh way, when I probably ought to simply relax and concentrate on clarity.

Now that I have made that confession, I feel better. Whether it helps you, the reader, or not is another question.

The central theme of each chapter will be rooted in a particular scripture. This is done deliberately to underscore Wesley's claim that he was a person of "one Book," and to call us Methodists back to the primary source of our life as individuals and in the church. A recovery of an emphasis upon scripture is one of the crucial needs in United Methodism.

I have also deliberately quoted Wesley frequently. We need to read Wesley more if we are going to be faithful to our heritage; but more, we need to read him in order to capture the same Spirit that controlled his life and brought revival to England and America. Yet, I have also sought to put the message in our contemporary setting and experiential need.

It is my prayer that this effort will make a contribution to the renewal of our church as we discover or rediscover the unique place we have in God's family. We need to recover that uniqueness, not to set us apart from others, but that we might be the people God wants us to be. God would be pleased, I think, if we would take up again, with commitment, zeal, and dependence upon the Holy Spirit, that mission which was declared when the Methodist movement first put its roots down in this new land: "to reform a continent and spread scriptural holiness across the land." A Bicentennial Celebration will have been for naught unless it gives us a new vision and thrusts us into the future as Spirit-filled and Spirit-led people.

MAXIE DUNNAM

# Introduction to the New Edition

The significant addition to this new edition is a study guide I have prepared for individual and group use. For each chapter I have devised a set of questions for personal reflection and a separate set of questions to guide group sharing.

The design is that you will not read this book at one sitting, or even over a period of a few days. I hope that you will take it slowly as you read each chapter, taking time to ponder and study the questions for personal reflection. Use the space provided at the end of each chapter to write your reflections when I ask you to do that. If you wish to write more extended answers, keep a separate notebook as your personal journal.

The Wesleyan expression of our Christian faith is experiential. Reading the book, and responding to the questions for personal reflection, will assist you in getting in touch with your own spiritual pilgrimage *experientially*.

There is a set of questions for each chapter to guide group sharing. If you use the book as a group study resource, these questions will be helpful in our regular discussion gatherings.

My suggestion is that the leader of the group (and leadership may change for each session) read the questions ahead of time and select the ones that should have priority in your particular group. Again, however, questions for each group meeting call for the sharing of personal *experience*, not just ideas and content. You will miss the potential richness of this adventure unless you give that priority. John Wesley said the meaning of Christian fellowship is one loving heart setting another on fire. We do that primarily by sharing our personal journeys.

Naturally I'm pleased that this book is being released now in a new format since it was originally published in 1984. I believe this will be the most *useful* format. My thanks to Craig Gallaway for his idea for this edition and for his persistent and supportive encouragement, and to Bishop William R. Cannon for his foreword.

MAXIE DUNNAM

# Chapter I
## *The Keystone: Salvation by Faith*

*You were dead through the trespasses and sins in which you once lived. . . . But God, who is rich in mercy, out of the great love with which he loved us even when we were dead through our trespasses, made us alive together with Christ—by grace you have been saved—and raised us up with him and seated us with him in the heavenly places in Christ Jesus, so that in the ages to come he might show the immeasurable riches of his grace in kindness toward us in Christ Jesus. For by grace you have been saved through faith, and this is not your own doing; it is the gift of God—not the result of works, so that no one may boast. For we are what he made us, created in Christ Jesus for good works, which God prepared beforehand to be our way of life* (Eph. 2:1, 2, 4-10).

If you were asked, "What is the goal of your life?" how would you respond? To be happy? To have a healthy, happy family? To be a success in business? To be wealthy? To serve other people and make others happy? To find the right marriage mate? To be fulfilled in your profession? Listen to the founder of Methodism, John Wesley.

To candid, reasonable men, I'm not afraid to lay open what have been the inmost thoughts of my heart. I have thought, I'm a creature of a day, passing through life as an arrow through the air. I am a spirit come from God, and returning to God: Just hovering over the great gulf; til a few moments hence, I am no more seen; I drop into an unchangeable eternity. I want to know one thing—the way to heaven; how to land safe on that happy shore. God himself has condescended to teach the way; for this very end He came from heaven. He hath written it down in a book. O give me that book! At any price, give me the Book of God! (*John Wesley's Fifty-Three Sermons,* edited by Edward H. Sugden [Nashville: Abingdon Press, 1983]. This quotation is taken from the Preface to the Sermons.)

This word expressed the fire burning in Wesley's soul: "I want to know one thing—the way to heaven—how to land safe on that happy shore." This desire of Wesley was like that passionate expression of Paul to the Philippians:

Not that I have already obtained this or have already reached the goal; but I press on to make it my own, because Christ Jesus has made me his own. Beloved, I do not consider that I have made it my own; but this one thing I do: forgetting what

1

lies behind and straining forward to what lies ahead, I press on toward the goal for the prize of the heavenly call of God in Christ Jesus (Phil. 3:12-14).

The goal of Wesley's life was his own salvation. History verifies that once he was certain of that—his own salvation—the passion became other-directed, and he started one of the great revivals of history as he sought to share the salvation message with others. Over and over in this *Journal,* he records his preaching activity in his simple sentence: "I offered them Christ."

John Wesley published four volumes of sermons—in 1746, 1748, 1750, and 1760. In 1763, he prepared a model deed for his preaching houses which set forth his intentions after his death. In that deed, it was provided that persons appointed by the conference should "have and enjoy the premises" only on condition "that the said persons preach no other doctrine than is contained in Mr. Wesley's Notes upon the New Testament and four volumes of sermons" (*John Wesley's Fifty-Three Sermons,* Ibid., p. 1).

"Salvation by faith" was the first of Wesley's *standard sermons.* So, this is where we begin, the keystone of his understanding of Christian doctrine—"salvation by faith."

Paul developed this theme systematically in his Letter to the Romans. His Galatian letter was an expression of the same truth primarily from his heart, not his head. Our scripture from Ephesians is a spontaneous outpouring of this conviction about salvation by faith in the midst of a commentary on the nature and mission of the church.

Since Paul, volumes have been written on this theme of salvation by faith; and I boldly propose to capture the essence of it (at least enough for us to go on) in this chapter by asking, in the style of Mr. Wesley's sermon on this theme, three questions:

One, who needs it?
Two, what is it we need?
Three, how do we get it?

## WHO NEEDS SALVATION?

First, who needs it? The answer is clear, simple, and encompassing: We all need it.

Paul stated our predicament: "You were dead through the trespasses and sins in which you once lived, following the course of this world, following the ruler of the power of the air, the spirit that is now at work among those who are disobedient" (Eph. 2:1-2).

In Romans 3, Paul deals specifically with the universality of sin, quoting passages from five psalms and one verse from Isaiah. Consider his terrible word:

"There is no one who is righteous, not even one;
  there is no one who has understanding,
  there is no one who seeks God.
All have turned aside, together they have become worthless;
  there is no one who shows kindness,
  there is not even one."
"Their throats are opened graves;
  they use their tongues to deceive."
"The venom of vipers is under their lips."
  "Their mouths are full of cursing and bitterness."
"Their feet are swift to shed blood;
  ruin and misery are in their paths,
and the way of peace they have not known."
  "There is no fear of God before their eyes."

(Rom. 3:10-18)

Paul begins this catalog of our common predicament by contending that we are all under sin. Think about that for a moment.

Charles Gatemouth Brown is one of America's foremost composers and singers of "blues" music. He is the recipient of a Grammy and won the W. T. Handy Blues Award in 1983. In an interview on ABC News, he said, "Anyone who has brains gets the blues."

That's universal, isn't it? Paul and John Wesley would express the same universal compass of sin: "Anyone who is human is a sinner."

In Romans 3:9, Paul contends that everyone, "both Jews and Greeks, are under the power of sin." The Greek phrase that Paul uses for this state of being under sin when we are without Christ is *hypo harmartian,* and it means "in the power of" or "under the authority of" sin. You get the scope of it by seeing the way Paul uses that phrase in other places: He described the relationship between a schoolboy and his teacher in Galatians 3:25 (KJV) as being "under a schoolmaster." In 1 Timothy 6:1, he said slaves were "under the yoke." In both these instances, to be "under" means to be dominated by or under the authority of.

That's the predicament of all of us. Paul summed it up: *"For there is no distinction, since all have sinned and fall short of the glory of God"* (Rom. 3:22-23).

Do you have problems believing that? Is the description Paul uses too terrible? In another chapter, we will deal with the whole issue of "original sin." For now, let's not debate the universality of sin, but seek to see where we are in the picture. Without dealing with such glaring sins as adultery, killing, and stealing, answer these questions:

—Do you sometimes think more highly of yourself than you ought to think?
—Is there any person of whom you are jealous?

4

—Do you occasionally look at a person of the opposite sex and feel lust in your heart?

—Do you sometimes hate people of other races or nations?

—Do you get anxious about the future because you feel you don't have enough financial security?

—Do you judge others by what they have? By their station in life? Whether they are cultured or not? Their level of educational achievement?

Now those questions sound innocent, don't they? And most of us would answer yes to a number of them. Do you know what that means? It means that we are among those Paul was describing: "All have sinned and fall short of the glory of God."

So who needs it? Who needs salvation? We all do!

## WHAT SALVATION DO WE NEED?

Now, the second question: What is it we need? We need salvation. What is the nature of this salvation?

Let's take our cue directly from scripture. Paul describes the result of sin in our life: "You were dead in trespasses and sins." You were not in control of your life—you followed "the course of this world" like a puppet controlled by Satan. This means that you lived in "the passion of your flesh, following the desires of body and mind."

But then something happened. God "made us alive together with Christ." It's a dramatic distinction. Sin equals death—you were dead; salvation equals life—God made us live. This is an echo of Paul's whole life. He knew himself to be a great sinner, but he knew Christ to be a great Savior. He never understated or underplayed sin in our lives; nor did he understate or underplay the redeeming power of Jesus Christ. So it was with John Wesley.

The salvation we need and the salvation Christ affords is the salvation from sin. Be clear about this. It is a *present* salvation. Paul did not say to the Ephesians, "You *will* be saved." He said, "You *have been* saved." The work is accomplished now. Let us see how this happens at the point of three great needs:

First, it is a salvation from *the guilt of all past sins*. Paul put it graphically in Colossians 2:1-14. We have been forgiven all our sins; "the record that stood against us with its legal demands" has been set aside, cancelled, *nailed to the cross*.

What a descriptive metaphor—nailed to the cross. Nothing can be more dramatic or powerful—to know that when Jesus was nailed to the cross, *our sin,* my sins, your sins, and the guilt therefrom was nailed to the cross. I see this demonstrated over and over again. Here is one picture of it:

A fifty-year-old woman—let's call her Mary—was devastated with guilt over estrangement from and hatred of her father. Mary's mother had died of cancer. During the last months of her mother's life, Mary's father had courted, and married almost immediately after the death of his wife, another woman. Mary's hatred for her father and his new wife was venomous. She refused to see or have anything to do with them. She finally came to see that hatred was destroying her. Then she became plagued with guilt over fifteen years of estrangement from her father. Her guilt paralyzed her. She wanted reconciliation but she could not take the initiative in the relationship. The father had given up long ago.

At the close of a worship service where the theme of forgiveness—salvation from all past sin and guilt—had been proclaimed, Mary and I shared and prayed together for about an hour. Mary believed, accepted the forgiveness of grace, and claimed salvation for herself. That very night she wrote to her father, and began the process of reconciliation and the reclaiming and rebuilding of a daughter-father love and relationship.

Second, we are saved not only from the guilt of all past sins; *we are also saved from fear.* Fear is the twin of guilt and burns almost as ravagingly as guilt itself in many of our lives—fear of God's judgment, of eternal punishment, of God's wrath.

But the salvation Christ affords takes away our fear. We now know not the wrath of God, but God's extravagant love. We "have not received the spirit of bondage again to fear . . . , but . . . the Spirit of adoption, whereby we cry, Abba, Father. The Spirit itself beareth witness with our spirit, that we are the children of God" (Rom. 8:15-16, KJV).

John Wesley would remind us that we are also saved from the fear, though not from the possibility, of falling away from the grace of God and coming short of God's great and precious promises. That is a unique understanding of Methodism. We will return to it later. We are saved from the fear, though not the possibility, of falling away from the grace of God. We are "sealed with the promised Holy Spirit, which is the guarantee of our inheritance" (Eph. 1:13, RSV).

That, too, is a unique understanding of Methodism. We are saved from the fear, though not the possibility, of falling away from the grace of God. So, we have peace with God through our Lord Jesus Christ. We rejoice in the hope of the glory of God, and the love of God is shed abroad in our hearts, through the Holy Spirit, which is given to us.

And hereby we are persuaded, though perhaps not at all times, nor with the same fullness of persuasion, that neither death nor life, nor things present nor things to come, nor height, nor depth, nor any creature shall be able to separate us from the love of God, which is in Christ Jesus our Lord.

We are saved from fear.

Third, the last word about the nature of our salvation is that we are *saved from the power of sin.* We will discuss this in the chapter on sanctification, but it must be noted now. Paul was very clear about the fact that unredeemed persons live under the power of sin. He was also triumphantly clear about the fact that Christ frees us from the power of sin. "He has rescued us from the power of darkness and transferred us into the kingdom of his beloved Son" (Col. 1:13). This was Wesley's deep conviction. Charles Wesley sang joyfully about this fact:

> Long my imprisoned spirit lay,
> Fast bound by sin and nature's night;
> Thine eye diffused a quickening ray,
> I woke, the dungeon flamed with light;
> My chains fell off, my heart was free.
> I rose, went forth, and followed thee.

*(The United Methodist Hynmal,* #363)

So, what is it we need? Salvation that is a present reality—salvation from sin, from the guilt and fear that result from sin, and from the power over us.


## HOW DO WE RECEIVE SALVATION?

Now, the final question: *How do we get it?* The answer is this: We don't get it; *it is given.*

Isn't it strange that we have as many problems with this fact as any other? One of the crucial debates of Christian doctrine has swirled around this issue. How are we to be saved? Two theories have been set forth as to how we are reconciled to God: one is by *works,* the other by *faith.* We underscore again Paul's words from Ephesians 2:8-9: "For by grace you have been saved through faith, and this is not your own doing; it is the gift of God—not the result of works, so that no one may boast." How do we get it? We don't; it is given. Salvation is by faith and faith alone.

In Romans 3:23-25, Paul states the truth about salvation as a gift in this fashion: "Since all have sinned and fall short of the glory of God, they are justified by his grace as a gift, through the redemption which is Christ Jesus, whom God put forward as an expiation by his blood, to be received by faith" (RSV). The Greek word for expiation "refers to the sacrifices offered to pagan deities, as a means of appeasing their displeasure and averting their anger." Some theologians transferred this concept to the New Testament and saw Christ's sacrifice as a means of placating an angry God. Others have objected to this interpretation on the grounds that it demeans God's nature, that it reduces God to the level of a petty pagan deity.

A different view emphasizes the fact that this word "is used in the Greek translation of the Old Testament to translate the phrase *Mercy Seat.* In Hebrew ritual, the high-priest appeared before the Ark of the Covenant, which contained the stone tablets of the Law. The priest sprinkled blood from a sacrifice on the golden lid of the Ark which was called the Mercy Seat. The symbolism richly portrayed the fact that a broken law stood between God and the people, but through the shedding of blood, the place of judgment and estrangement became the place of mercy and reconciliation. Christ's death is therefore seen as the means whereby God's demand for justice against a sinful race is fully met, thereby freeing God to be merciful to those who formally merited only judgment." (See D. Stuart Briscoe, *The Communicator's Commentary, Romans,* pp. 93-94.)

Now, a picture from the human scene that will help us understand this magnificent truth: One of the most beautiful and moving love stories I have ever heard is that of Thomas Moore, the nineteenth century Irish poet. Shortly after his marriage, he was called away on business. It was some time before he returned home, and when he did, he found waiting for him at the front door of the house, not his beautiful bride, but the family doctor.

"Your wife is upstairs," said the doctor, "but she's asked that you do not come up." Then Thomas Moore learned the terrible truth: His wife had contracted smallpox. The disease had left her once flawless skin pocked and scarred. She had taken one look at her reflection in the mirror and had commanded the shutters be drawn and that her husband never see her again.

Moore would not listen. He ran upstairs and opened the door to his wife's room. It was black as night inside. Not a sound came from the darkness. Groping along the wall, Moore grasped for the gas jets.

A startled cry came from the black corner of the room. "No! Don't light the lamps!"

Moore hesitated, swayed by the pleading in the voice. "Go!" she begged, "Please go! This is the greatest gift I can give you now."

Moore did go. He went down to his study where he sat up most of the night, prayerfully writing—not a poem this time, but a song. He had never written a song before, but now it seemed more in keeping with his mood than simply poetry. He not only wrote the words, he wrote the music too. The next morning as soon as the sun was up, he returned to his wife's room. He felt his way to a chair and sat down. "Are you awake?" he asked.

"I am," came a voice from the far side of the room. "But you must not ask to see me. You must not press me, Thomas."

"I will sing to you, then," he answered. And so for the first time, Thomas Moore sang to his wife the song that still lives today:

> Believe me, if all those endearing young charms,
> which I gaze on so fondly today,
> Were to change by tomorrow and flee from my arms,
> like fairy gifts fading away,

> Thou wouldst still be adored, as this moment thou art,
> Let thy loveliness fade as it will . . .

He heard a movement from the dark corner where his wife lay in her loneliness, waiting. He continued:

> Let thy loveliness fade as it will,
> and round the dear ruin each wish of my heart
> Would entwine itself verdantly still.

The song ended. As his voice trailed off the last note, Moore heard his bride arise. She crossed the room to the window, reached up, and slowly drew open the shutters. That's the power of love. And that is only a hint of the love of Christ for us.

We don't deserve that love. We can't earn it. It is given. Ravaged by the guilt and fear that result from this dreadful disease, pocked and scarred as we are by sin, we hear the love song of God: "Indeed, God did not send the Son into the world to condemn the world, but in order that the world might be saved through him" (John 3:17). We see that music translated into the sacrificial action of Christ on the cross. To this place of extravagant love and mercy we come. Believing that Christ died for us, miraculously the shutters are opened upon our dark world of sin, guilt, and fear. Our lives are flooded with the light of God's salvation, and God makes us "alive together with Christ," forever freed from the bondage of sin.

That is the keystone of Wesley's doctrine—salvation by faith—and it is all rooted in God's grace, which is the theme of our next chapter.

## QUESTIONS FOR PERSONAL REFLECTION

1. For John Wesley, the goal of "getting to heaven" was a matter of highest priority (page 1). List four or five goals of your life. Then, as you begin this study, honestly describe where the goal of "getting to heaven" fits into your overall goals.

2. On pages 3-4 is a set of questions that help to illustrate the universality of sin and the need for salvation. Answer each of these questions specifically. What do your answers tell you about your own need for salvation?

3. Spend some time reflecting on your life. Are there more glaring or destructive "sins" than the ones listed in the questions?

4. In your own words, describe what it means to say that we are *saved by faith.*

5. Christ saves us from the *guilt* of sin (page 4). Is there a burden of guilt in your life for which you have not accepted Christ's forgiveness? Write a brief description of any burden that you can identify.

If you are still struggling with guilt, consider sharing this with a trusted friend or pastor, asking for prayer for relief of the burden. Name the person(s) with whom you would be willing to share. Make plans to contact one of these persons immediately.

6. Salvation in Christ also saves us from two forms of fear: the fear of God's judgment (eternal punishment) and the fear that we might fall away from the grace of God (page 5). Do you struggle with either of these forms of fear? Briefly describe these or any other fears that continue to challenge your faith.

7. The essence of the Wesleyan understanding of faith can be summed up in the statement: *In the cross, Christ did something for you that you can never do for yourself.* In your own words, describe what Christ did, and write a paragraph expressing your gratitude for Christ's work in your life.

## QUESTIONS FOR GROUP SHARING

1. Discuss the notion of "getting to heaven" as a primary goal of life. Ask persons who are willing to share where this goal fits into their overall life goals.

2. Discuss what is meant by the universality of sin.

3. Invite as many persons as will share their personal experiences of salvation from the *guilt,* the *fear,* and/or the *power* of sin.

4. Discuss the fact that salvation is a *present* reality, not simply a future hope.

5. Invite the group to respond to this statement: "In the cross, Christ did something for us that we can never do ourselves."

# Chapter II
## *Amazing Grace*

*For God so loved the world that he gave his only Son, so that everyone who believes in him may not perish but may have eternal life. Indeed, God did not send the Son into the world to condemn the world, but in order that the world might be saved through him. Those who believe in him are not condemned; but those who do not believe are condemned already, because they have not believed in the name of the only Son of God. And this is the judgment, that the light has come into the world, and people loved darkness rather than light because their deeds were evil* (John 3:16-19).

*But now, apart from law, the righteousness of God has been disclosed, and is attested by the law and the prophets, the righteousness of God through faith in Jesus Christ for all who believe. For there is no distinction, since all have sinned and fall short of the glory of God; they are now justified by his grace as a gift, through the redemption that is in Christ Jesus, whom God put forward as a sacrifice of atonement by his blood, effective through faith. He did this to show his righteousness, because in his divine forbearance he had passed over the sins previously committed; it was to prove at the present time that he himself is righteous and that he justifies the one who has faith in Jesus* (Rom. 3:21-26).

The proclamation of the Christian gospel is not restricted to pulpits and Sunday school classrooms. The January 9, 1984, issue of *Time* magazine carried on its cover a full-color picture of Pope John Paul II and his would-be killer Mehmet Ali Agca. The Pope is shaking Ali Agca's hand, and his other hand is around Agca's shoulder. A one-inch type insert spans the picture, drawing the two men even closer together. The bold question of the print is WHY FORGIVE?

The cover story was excellent, proclaiming with evangelical zeal that a pardon from the Pontiff was a lesson in forgiveness in a troubled world.

Most readers of the magazine had probably forgotten the story of the attempted assassination which had taken place in Rome's St. Peter's Square in May 1981. Violence is so common. Spectacles of revenge and terror occur so regularly that we pass them off almost as soon as they happen.

But when it happened, it shocked the world as the picture was captured on TV and in newspapers. Pope John Paul II, in white robes, was capsized backward on his seat, stricken, in a posture reminiscent of the *Pieta*. There was a dramatic burst of emotion and shock in the scene as the security personnel sprang alive and the Pontiff's white "popemobile" lurched off through the crowd. The Pope had been shot.

Ordinarily, a spasm of savagery such as that simply passes and recedes in time— an ugly, vague memory, if recalled at all. But in an extraordinary moment of grace, the memory of that violence in St. Peter's Square was transformed. *Time* magazine told the story:

> In a bare white-walled cell in Rome's Rebibbia Prison, John Paul tenderly held the hand that had held the gun that was meant to kill him. For twenty-one minutes the Pope sat with his would-be assassin Mehmet Ali Agca. The two talked softly. Once or twice, Ali Agca laughed. The Pope forgave him for the shooting. At the end of the meeting, Agca either kissed the Pope's ring or pressed the Pope's hand to his forehead in a Moslem gesture of relief.

> It was a startling drama of forgiveness and reconciliation. The Pope spoke in whispers but he also meant to proclaim a message to the world. The only other people in the cell with Agca and John Paul were the Pope's personal secretary, two security agents—and a Vatican photographer and television crew. The Roman Catholic Church for many centuries has used imagery—paintings, sculpture, architecture—to express its spiritual meanings. The Pope brought the photographer and the cameramen because he wanted the image in that cell to be shown around a world filled with nuclear arsenals and unforgiving hatreds.

> It is difficult to imagine a more perfect economy of drama. The Pope's *deed* spoke, not his words, and it spoke with the full authority of his mortal life and the danger to which Agca had subjected it. The meaning of John Paul's forgiveness was profoundly Christian. He embraced his enemy and pardoned him (*Time,* Jan. 9, 1984, pp. 28-29).

It was a moving picture of grace which was the primary theme of John Wesley, Philip William Otterbein, and Jacob Albright. It is a core belief for the United Methodist Christian.

*Time* magazine is not unaware of the power of pictures and the dramatic use of imagery. The magnificent article was punctuated with pictures, photographic vignettes, that set the question, "Why forgive?" deep in the stark reality of violence that is the signature of a world gone mad. There was the picture of the Pope when he was shot, held from collapsing by another person. There was a picture of Beirut in the chaotic aftermath of a terrorist car bomb explosion; the eyes of the closest man in the picture portray a haunting terror that comes either from paralyzing fear or raging anger. There was also a picture of a shabby, bare room of the Sabra Refugee Camp in Lebanon; stretched out on the cold, dirty floor of that room was the lifeless body of a pregnant Palestinian woman.

There were other pictures—but one was missing. The drama of grace and forgiveness would have been complete with a picture of Calvary—three crosses against a dark, stormy sky, with Jesus hanging on the center one, struggling to speak that final word of grace, "Father, forgive them."

Grace—amazing grace—it is the heart of the Christian gospel. John captured it in this encompassing word: "For God so loved the world that he gave his only Son, so that everyone who believes in him may not perish but may have eternal life. God did not send the Son into the world to condemn the world, but in order that the world might be saved through him."

And this is what Paul argued about so convincingly with the Romans: "Since all have sinned and fall short of the glory of God; they are now justified by his grace as a gift, through the redemption that is in Christ Jesus, whom God put forward as a sacrifice of atonement by his blood, effective through faith" (Rom. 3:23-25).

John Wesley did us a great service and provided us with a distinctive emphasis by talking about grace impinging upon us and working in three specific ways: prevenient grace, justifying grace, and sanctifying grace. Prevenient grace is the grace of God going before us, pulling us, wooing us, seeking to open our minds and hearts, and eventually giving us faith. Justifying grace is the forgiving love of God, freely given to us, reconciling us, putting us right with God, making Christ, who knew no sin, to be sin on our behalf. Sanctifying grace is the work and spirit of Christ within us, restoring the broken image, completing the salvation which was begun in justification, and bringing us to complete newness of life and perfection in love.

We will discuss sanctifying grace in Chapter Four. Here we will look at prevenient and justifying grace.

## PREVENIENT GRACE

I have a picture in my office—a painting by my wife, Jerry. You have to study many paintings to get their meaning, and sometimes the meaning you get is not what the artist intended. I heard of a person who went into a museum of modern art. Looking around at what to him was a horrid onslaught of color and distorted design, he commented, "There is less here than meets the eye."

Now my wife doesn't paint that way, but this piece is an impressionistic design of color and movement, dominantly blue, from deep shades to translucent light. The person in this painting, engulfed in the flow of color, is not obvious at first glance, but is distinct when really studied. The person stands in the swirl of color and movement surrounded by light and life that comes from somewhere beyond; yet you know it is this light and movement that is energizing and giving the person life.

Jerry called her painting "Grace" because it is the expression of her experience of God's love as proclaimed in the hymn, "I Sought the Lord." At a particular time of struggle in her life, the hymn ministered to her, and her painting flowed from that experience.

I sought the Lord, and afterward I knew
He moved my soul to seek him, seeking me.
It was not I that found, O Savior true;
No, I was found of thee.

Thou didst reach forth thy hand and mine enfold;
I walked and sank not on the storm-vexed sea.
'Twas not so much that I on thee took hold,
As thou, dear Lord, on me.

*(The United Methodist Hymnal, #341)*

That's the nature of prevenient grace. The Lord seeks us before we begin to seek. Wesley sounded this note strongly in opposition to a doctrine of predestination. Whether the rigid, double predestination idea—that some are damned to hell while others are elected for heaven, or another variation on that theme—the doctrine of predestination has as its center an understanding of grace as limited. For Wesley—and this is another particularly United Methodist emphasis—grace is universal. It is "free in all, and free for all." Bishop William R. Cannon makes the case.

To be sure, it is free to all in the sense that it is given without price, that it does not demand anything of us before it is bestowed, and that it flows from the free mercy of God. But note the change. Grace is free *for all*. It is not free only for those whom God has ordained to life, but it is like the air we breathe, or the wind that blows in our faces; it is for everyone who dwells upon the face of the earth (*The Theology of John Wesley,* p. 93).

Now that doesn't mean that all persons receive this grace, or that they deliberately appropriate it, or respond to it for their salvation. They don't. That is the reason we began with the emphasis on faith in the first chapter. For salvation we must respond in faith to God's grace. But let's continue looking specifically at the nature of God's amazing grace.

Prevenient grace (or "preventing grace") is the *grace that comes before.* Now what does that mean? It means that before any conscious personal experience of divine grace, grace is there, working in our lives even before we are aware of it. The first move is God's, not ours. This is the witness of the scripture. As clear as anything else in the Bible is the fact that God seeks us. God is, as Francis Thompson would say, "the hound of heaven" who relentlessly pursues us. That's the story over and over again in the Bible—a searching God who takes the initiative in human life.

It all began with Adam and Eve in the garden. When they had sinned, they experienced guilt. They did not want to see God, or for God to see them, so they hid. But God came looking for them, calling them by name, "Adam, Eve, where are you?"

Moses hid from God in Midian. He didn't want God to find him because he knew what God was going to ask him to do.

The story goes on: Elijah hiding in a cave. Peter trying to hide his Galilean accent from those around the fire in the courtyard where Jesus was on trial.

That is the story: people hiding, God seeking. Jesus underscored it with the three parables Luke put together for "the gospel in the Gospel"—the parables of the lost coin, the lost sheep, and the lost son. That's the point of view of the Bible, what the scripture is all about—the story of God searching for us. Most of us thought it was the other way around, didn't we? We thought the Bible was the story about people who were looking for God. That really isn't so. It's the story of God seeking us.

In his underscoring of prevenient grace, Wesley echoed Peter's word that God is "not wanting any to perish, but all to come to repentance" (2 Pet. 3:9).

Prevenient grace is not only "the grace that comes before," meaning that God takes the first step in our redemption; it is a *leading grace*. It is the activity of the Spirit in our lives, moving us to a place of repentance and reconciliation.

Wesley noted three ways in which prevenient grace leads us. One, it creates in us our first sensitivity to God's call, to God's seeking us, to God's will. Two, it produces an awareness and conviction that we have violated God's will and are not responsive to the divine call. Now this conviction may be slight and transient, but it is real and is a part of God's prevenient grace working in us. Three, prevenient grace stimulates our first wish to please God.

These three workings of prevenient grace in our lives, according to Wesley, lead us to repentance which is a necessary step to salvation. It is important to underscore what we noted earlier. God's grace is universal, but prevenient grace is not sufficient for salvation. A person may suppress or ignore this grace. If so, scripture warns that we may experience hardness of heart, so that these stirrings of the Spirit within will go unheeded. We will look at this again when we discuss free will and predestination in the next chapter.

Review a bit. Wesley said grace is "free in all, and free for all." No one is excluded from the work of prevenient grace. Grace is *for all*, a gift from God. But prevenient grace must be responded to in order for us to experience its justifying power.

## JUSTIFYING GRACE

The resounding word of the New Testament is that we are justified by grace. That's good news!

Have you heard the story of the man who came home one night feeling very sorry for himself? Nothing had gone right at the office. It was one of those days when there seemed to be one hassle after another. When he arrived home, he could tell by the look on his wife's face that she had probably had the same kind of day. Before she could say anything, he said, "I don't know what your day has been like, and I don't know what you're getting ready to tell me, but if it's bad news, please keep it to yourself. I've had all the bad news I can stand for one day."

She looked at him with some uncertainty, and then said, "Well, maybe it is good news. You know we have six wonderful children." He said, "That's right." Then she said, "You'll be happy to know that five of them did not break an arm today."

Good news or bad news is sometimes a matter of perspective. The bad news of our life is that we have all sinned and fallen short of the glory of God. The good news is that God is gracious, and while we deserve condemnation, we are justified. God delivers us. We are saved by grace.

*Justification* is the common word used to describe what God does freely for us through grace. It is a metaphor primarily from the law courts. Keep in mind the supreme question: How can we as sinners get into a right relationship with God? How are we able to feel at peace, at ease, at home, with God? How can we escape the feeling of fear in the presence of God—the sense of estrangement, of judgment? That's the problem. Judaism answered the questions this way: A person can attain a right relationship with God by keeping the law. By fulfilling all the works of the law, a person will be right with God. But condemnation is implicit in this, for no one can live in perfect obedience, keeping every law. So, salvation is not a way of works, but a way of faith.

Justification is based on the imagery of being on trial before God. *Diakioun* is the Greek word translated "to justify." William Barclay provides helpful insight into this word. All Greek verbs which end in *-oun* mean not to *make* someone something, but to *treat,* to *reckon,* or to *account* someone as something. The point about God's relationship to us is this: When we appear before God, we are anything but innocent; we are utterly guilty. Yet God *treats* us, *reckons* us, *accounts* us as if we were innocent. That is what justification means.

When Paul says that "God justifies the ungodly," he means that God, in incredible mercy, treats us as if we were godly people. This is what shocked the Jews. To treat a bad man as if he were a good man was the sign of a wicked judge. "He that justifieth the wicked, and he that condemneth the just, even they both are abomination to the Lord" (Prov. 17:15, KJV). "I will not justify the wicked" (Ex. 23:7, KJV). But Paul says that is precisely what God does. (See William Barclay, *The Daily Study Bible: The Letter to the Romans,* p. 54.)

Though justification is a metaphor of the law court, we cannot understand the grace of God justifying us unless we see sin, not as a crime against law, but as a crime against love. To be sure, in sin we break God's law, but more important, we break God's heart. We may atone for a broken law, but how do we atone for a broken heart?

We have a painting in our bedroom that would not be considered great art, but one that has profound meaning for us. It was painted by a friend who was a member of one of our former congregations. The painting is of a little black girl with haunting eyes that reflect a mixture of sadness and hope. Mary Jo started painting as therapy for the deep sorrow of her life. It was one of her first paintings.

One afternoon, she and her three daughters were at the shopping center which was within walking distance of their home. She was carrying the baby, and the other two little blonde, blue-eyed girls were walking along where they should have been—ahead of her on the sidewalk. It happened without warning. An elderly man coming out of a parking place bumped another car, panicked, and hit the gas pedal instead of the brake. The car jumped the curb, crashed into one of the little girls, and threw her through the guard rail along the sidewalk and into a ravine below. She was dead—before her mother's eyes.

I don't know what happened to the driver. Drivers whose carelessness or recklessness takes lives are usually arrested, tried, found guilty, fined, sometimes imprisoned, their driver's license suspended. But after such persons have paid their fines or served their sentences, the law has no further claim upon them. As far as the law is concerned, justice has been served. The matter is over.

But that doesn't touch the issue of the parents' hearts whose child has been killed, or the heart of the driver himself. The driver of the car that snuffed out the life of our little friend could never make things up to her parents, never put things right by serving a sentence or paying a fine. Love—parent-love—had ended in a heartbreak for all, and only the forgiveness of the little girl's parents could mend the relationship between them and the driver.

That is the way it is in our relationship with God. We may have broken God's laws, but the terrible tragedy is that we've broken God's heart. Only an act of the free forgiveness of God's grace can bring us back into relationship with God. And that's what the cross is all about—*amazing grace,* justifying us.

I think about that amazing grace when I look at Mary Jo's painting. She forgave the man who killed their child and worked out her grief by painting the likeness of little children from all over the world. The little black girl in our bedroom is one of those children. As I look into her sad but hopeful eyes, I am reminded that God is saddened by our sinfulness, but hopeful—always hopeful that none of us will perish but that all of us will come to repentance.

There is so much at the heart of what we United Methodists believe to be the core of the gospel and Christian experience that we need to look longer at this justifying aspect of grace. We do so by focusing on Paul's word: "Since all have sinned and fall short of the glory of God; they are now justified by his grace as a gift, through the redemption that is in Christ Jesus, whom God put forward as a sacrifice of atonement by his blood, effective through faith" (Rom. 3:23-25).

Paul uses three metaphors in this passage that help us understand justifying grace. The first is *justification,* the metaphor from the law courts which we have already discussed. Before God's court, we are utterly guilty. Yet, in amazing mercy, God *treats* us, *reckons* us, *accounts* us as innocent. When we believe that God loves us, that Christ died for us, and when we trust God's loving activity in Jesus Christ for our salvation, we are justified.

That leads to the second metaphor, that of *sacrifice*. Paul says God put forward Jesus Christ as a propitiation (or expiation) for our sin. The Greek word translated as *propitiation* or *expiation* has to do with sacrifice. This was prominent in the Old Testament, but also present in most religions. To appease God, sacrifices were offered. These were efforts to avert the wrath of God. The pattern in the Old Testament was the offering of animal sacrifices. But even in the Old Testament, there are the stirrings that such were not adequate. David stated it clearly out of the anguish of his own sin and guilt: "For you have no delight in sacrifice; if I were to give a burnt offering, you would not be pleased. The sacrifice acceptable to God is a broken spirit; a broken and contrite heart, O God, you will not despise" (Ps. 51:16-17). Likewise Micah made the case: "With what shall I come before the Lord, and bow myself before God on high? Shall I come before him with burnt offerings, with calves a year old? Will the Lord be pleased with thousands of rams, with ten thousands of rivers of oil? Shall I give my firstborn for my transgression, the fruit of my body for the sin of my soul?" (Micah 6:6-7).

Paul concluded that only one sacrifice was sufficient—the sacrifice Jesus made on the cross. That sacrifice alone can atone and open the door to God that no other effort or action can accomplish.

The third metaphor Paul uses is taken from slavery. He speaks of the redemption, or deliverance, which is in Christ Jesus. The Greek word is *apolutrōsis* and means a ransoming, a redeeming, a liberating. It means that we are in the power, the grip, the dominion of sin; Christ alone can free us.

Now none of these metaphors alone is adequate. All of them together still do not probe the depth of the mystery. It is the mystery of what God does for us in Jesus Christ that we cannot do ourselves. It is justifying us when we are utterly guilty, providing a sacrifice when we have nothing to offer, setting us free when we are powerless to break the strong tentacles of sin. Wesley provides a good summary of it:

This then is the salvation which is through faith, even in the present world: a salvation from sin, and the consequences of sin, both often expressed in the word *justification;* which, taken in the largest sense, implies a deliverance from guilt and punishment, by the atonement of Christ actually applied to the soul of the sinner now believing on Him, and a deliverance from the (whole body) of sin, through Christ *formed in his heart.* So, that he who is thus justified, or saved by faith, is indeed *born again.* He is *born again of the Spirit* into a new life, which "is hid with Christ in God." (He is a new creature: old things are passed away: all things in him are become new.) And as a newborn babe, he gladly receives the . . . *"sincere* milk of the word, and grows thereby"; going on in the might of the Lord his God, from faith to faith, from grace to grace, until at length, he comes unto "a perfect man, unto the measure of the stature of the fullness of Christ" (*Fifty-Three Sermons,* p. 23).

In the next chapter we will look specifically at the power of sin in our lives, the sin from which we are freed. Then in Chapter Four we will return to Wesley's theme song, *grace,* as we consider sanctifying grace, or Christian perfection.

## *QUESTIONS FOR PERSONAL REFLECTION*

1. Recall your most vivid experience of forgiveness—of being forgiven or of forgiving another. Write enough about that experience to relive it in your mind.

2. Recall an example of God's prevenient grace in your life—the knowledge, in retrospect, that God was seeking you or leading you before you were aware of or had ackowledged God's grace (page 16). Make enough notes to get the experience clearly in mind.

3. Can you recall when you became aware of the fact that God's grace is "free in all, and free for all"?

4. Sin is not simply a crime against law; it is a crime against love (page 18). Can you recall a personal experience, your own or someone else's, where a "crime against love" was forgiven? Describe that experience.

5. The Apostle Paul used three metaphors to describe the meaning and significance of our justification in Christ—(1) being reckoned innocent in a court of law, (2) being reconciled through sacrifice, and (3) being set free from slavery (pages 19-20). Which of these is most descriptive of your own experience of justification? Why?

## QUESTIONS FOR GROUP SHARING

1. Invite two or three persons to share their most vivid experiences of being forgiven or of forgiving another.

2. Invite two or three persons to share how prevenient grace has worked specifically in their lives.

3. Discuss Wesley's idea of *universal grace* in light of Bishop Cannon's descriptive phrase, "free in all, free for all."

4. Discuss what difference it makes to see sin as a crime against love rather than simply as a crime against law.

5. Invite persons to share their experiences of justification in terms of the three metaphors that Paul uses. Are all three metaphors represented in the group's experiences?

# Chapter III
## *Sin: There's Nothing Original About It!*

*Did that which is good, then, bring death to me? By no means! It was sin, working death in me through what is good, in order that sin might be shown to be sin, and through the commandment might become sinful beyond measure. For we know that the law is spiritual; but I am of the flesh, sold into slavery under sin. I do not understand my own actions. For I do not do what I want, but I do the very thing I hate. Now if I do what I do not want, I agree that the law is good. But in fact it is no longer I that do it, but sin that dwells within me. For I know that nothing good dwells within me, that is, in my flesh. I can will what is right, but I cannot do it. For I do not do the good I want, but the evil I do not want is what I do. Now if I do what I do not want, it is no longer I that do it, but sin that dwells within me. So I find it to be a law that when I want to do what is good, evil lies close at hand. For I delight in the law of God in my inmost self, but I see in my members another law at war with the law of my mind, making me captive to the law of sin that dwells in my members. Wretched man that I am! Who will deliver me from this body of death? Thanks be to God through Jesus Christ our Lord! So then, with my mind, I am a slave to the law of God, but with my flesh I am a slave to the law of sin. There is therefore now no condemnation for those who are in Christ Jesus. For the law of the Spirit of life in Christ Jesus has set you free from the law of sin and death* (Rom. 7:13-8:2).

Somewhere along the way I heard of a little Christian college in Arkansas that advertised in its bulletin that it was sixteen miles from any known sin.

Now I grew up in the backwoods of Mississippi, and I know that Arkansas and Mississippi are a lot alike. But nowhere in my backwoods Mississippi could you get six miles, much less sixteen, from any known sin. Sin is not in a place, and you can't get away from it. Sin is in the person.

In this chapter we will look at the root of all human problems. The great majority of theologians talk about original sin. The fact is, there's nothing original about sin!

Think about that for a moment: There's nothing original about sin. What is the worst thing you've ever done in your life? Or, what have you done in the past month that you would label sinful? What led you to do that? Do you think you are the first person ever to act, feel, or relate in the fashion you are labeling sinful? There's nothing *original* about sin.

Augustine is one of the premier theologians of all times. In his classic book,

*Confessions,* he told the story of his youthful escapades of stealing pears from a neighbor's tree. He recorded that late one night a group of youngsters went out to "shake down and rob this tree." They took great loads of fruit from it "not for our own eating but rather to throw to the pigs." He went on to berate himself for the depth of sin this revealed. "The fruit gathered, I threw away, devouring in it only iniquity. There was no other reason, but foul was the evil, and I loved it."

Now why would one harmless prank such as this loom so large in Augustine's mind? By his own admission, he had taken a mistress, fathered a child out of wedlock, and indulged in every fleshly passion. Surely any of these was more serious than stealing pears.

Augustine saw in the "pear incident" his true nature and the nature of all humankind: In each of us there is sin. Some would soften this and say that within each of us there is the *susceptibility* to sin. But Wesley, in the train of Paul and Augustine, would say sin is there—not just a proneness to it, but sin itself. Since Adam, sin has been a part of every human life.

In this chapter, we will deal with the question of "original sin." But also, in light of the preceding chapters on salvation by faith, and prevenient and justifying grace, we will look at two other core concerns of a United Methodist Christian: predestination and freedom, and regeneration and the new birth.

## SIN IS UNIVERSAL

John Wesley talked more about the *universality* of sin than he did about "original sin." I think he did this because he was not willing to go as far as Augustine, for instance, on the total depravity of human nature. But he wasn't far from that position. He believed in "total depravity," but as Gilbert Rowe put it, not in "teetotal depravity." This was so because of Wesley's emphasis on grace. That's the reason we dealt with grace in the preceding chapter.

Recall that we said grace is universal, not limited. In Wesley's word, grace is "free in all, and free for all." About that there was no question. Wesley was as pessimistic about human nature as one could be, but there was a kind of optimism in his pessimism. Somewhere I saw a cartoon of a bum sitting on a park bench; his clothes were tattered and torn, his toes were coming out of his shoes—the stereotypical hobo-type. Beneath the picture was the caption: "No man is completely worthless— he can always serve as a horrible example."

Wesley knew himself and all human beings to be sinners, and we need to come to grips with that. But—and this is the rhythm and balance that is unique to Wesleyan theology—he was optimistic about grace. God's grace is sufficient. The power of sin is overcome by the power of God's love, mercy, and forgiveness. So John Wesley would join in the joyful triumphant cry of the Apostle Paul: "Where sin increased, grace abounded all the more" (Rom. 5:20). Because of prevenient grace, universally bestowed by God, our freedom to respond to God is always guaranteed. We'll come back to this in a moment; for now, return to sin. (Now I don't mean that literally, though that is the human pattern; we're constantly returning to sin!)

Have you read about the small town of Centralia, Pennsylvania? It's a mining town. More than twenty years ago, a fire broke out in the labyrinthian maze of tunnels and shafts which honeycomb the earth beneath the town. First the local, then the state, and now federal mine officials have tried to put the fire out. They have done everything they know, but it just keeps burning. Now and then a puff of smoke will break through the surface just to let everyone know the fire is still there.

Sin is like that. It is not always rampant in our lives, though it often is. It's there— and there's nothing original about it.

The text for Wesley's sermon on original sin was Genesis 6:5: "The Lord saw that the wickedness of humankind was great in the earth, and that every inclination of the thoughts of their hearts was only evil continually." Wesley laid the foundation for his sermon on original sin by sweeping quotations from scripture.

> The scripture avers, that "by one man's disobedience all men were constituted sinners"; that "in Adam, all died," spiritually died, lost the life and image of God; that fallen, sinful Adam then "begat a son in his own likeness"—nor was it possible he should beget him in any other; for "who can bring a clean thing out of unclean?"—That consequently we, as well as other men, were by nature "dead in trespasses and sin, without hope, without God in the world," and, therefore, "children of wrath"; that every man may say, "I was shapen in wickedness, and in sin did my mother conceive me"; that "there is no difference," in that "all have sinned and come short of the glory of God," of that glorious image of God wherein man was originally created. And hence, when the Lord looked down from heaven upon the children of men, He saw they were all gone out of the way; that they were altogether become abominable, there was none righteous, no, not one, "none that truly sought after God" (*Fifty-Three Sermons*, p. 558).

The scripture passage with which we began this chapter is no isolated word from Paul. It is the witness of scripture that with anguish Paul pours out in a personal confession. Is there a more poignant expression of the civil war raging within? "For I know that nothing good dwells within me, that is, in my flesh. I can will what is right, but I cannot do it. . . . Wretched man that I am! Who will deliver me from this body of death?" (Rom. 7:18-20, 21-24). What a raging fire of conscience! What a gripping heartcry! How often do we feel that ripping inside, the tearing apart of our efforts to be whole and centered and headed in a clear direction!

It is not only a personal problem; it happens in the whole of society. During World War I, Karl Barth was the pastor of a village church in Switzerland. A great darkness had descended upon Europe. Seemingly all the lights had gone out. Barth's people were crying for some word from the Lord that would make sense out of what had happened. Barth, however, had been raised in the nineteenth century and trained in its optimistic humanism, therefore he had nothing to preach. In desperation he turned to the scripture and discovered what he called "the strange new world within the Bible." Out of that experience, he wrote a book entitled *The Word of God and the Word of Man*. What Barth found in the Bible was strange because it described a world unlike the image of the world held by the confident liberals of the nineteenth century. When he came to Paul's letter to the Romans, Barth found there a diagnosis of the human condition that offered a reason for the chaos of his time.

The beginning point for Paul is stark realism about sin. He rejects, out of hand, the idea that sin is something we can get rid of with proper upbringing, or good education, or healthy environment, or evolutionary development, or cultural growth and planned development of civilization. Sin is at the very heart of our lives—in fact, sin lies beneath the surface of our lives and penetrates to the very core. That's what we mean when we talk about original sin. And there's nothing original about it because we are all infected by it.

So don't be naive about sin in your life, Paul would say—and likewise, Wesley and the early Methodists. The Duchess of Buckingham complained to the Countess of Huntingdon about this radical doctrine of sin being preached by the early Methodist preachers, and received this reply from the countess: "I thank your Ladyship for the information concerning the Methodist preachers. Their doctrines are most repulsive and strongly tinctured with impertinence and disrespect toward their superiors, in perpetually endeavoring to level all ranks and do away with all distinctions. It is monstrous to be told that you have a heart as sinful as the common wretches that crawl the earth" (W.E.H. Lecky, *A History of England in the 18th Century,* New Edition [London: Longmans, Green & Company, 1892], III, p. 122).

There are those in our day who still think it impertinent and repulsive to talk about sin in this fashion. For them, the problems of society and personal misery are located not in our alienation from God—not in our sin—but somewhere else. Our ignorance, not sin, is the problem. Psychological maladjustment, not sin, is our dilemma. Our surroundings are what "get to us"—not sin. Our feeling of power-lessness—not sin—that's the reason we're so impotent in living effectively in the world. Our economic inequities, our limited education, the inequality among persons—not sin—that's what is driving this country mad. So, if we improve education, if we cultivate self-understanding, if we raise everybody's standard of living, if we arrange proper socialization—then people will be saved and will be happy and fulfilled. Evil will disappear, and the problems of the world will be solved.

So, we tend to want to leave sin to the rescue missions, to the fundamentalist sects, to TV evangelists. Sin doesn't fit in our enlightened age of self-actualization, social engineering, positive thinking, and the delusion of "I'm OK, You're OK."

I think Wesley would laugh at us. He insisted that belief in a doctrine of universal sin is "the first distinguishing point between heathenism and Christianity. . . . Is man by nature filled with all manner of evil? Is he void of all good? Is he wholly fallen? Is his soul totally corrupted? . . . Allow this and you are so far a Christian. Deny it and you are heathen still" (Albert Outler, *Theology in the Wesleyan Spirit,* p. 37).

Now this is a grim picture, but the Gospels, the Apostle Paul, and Wesley have a saving word for us. In his understanding of sin, Wesley took a position between the extreme of tee-total depravity—in which we are utterly and hopelessly sinful, the image of God within having been obliterated—and the naive contention that we are able to sin or not to sin as we choose.

Wesley condemned the latter, the notion that we are able to sin or not sin as we please. Scripture and experience argue convincingly against the possibility that we can banish sin from our lives and from society if we can simply muster up sufficient moral effort and courage.

But Wesley also refused to go to the other extreme of Calvin: that with the image of God within us obliterated, we are utterly and hopelessly sinful. Instead of seeing sin as an obliteration of the image of God within us, he saw it as a *malignant disease* that could be cured only by the powerful grace of God. And this brings us to talk about predestination and free will.

## PREDESTINATION OR FREEDOM?

The extreme diagnosis of the human condition—that we are tee-totally depraved—has it that the image of God has been completely obliterated by Adam's fall. There is no way to change that. Thus comes the doctrine of *predestination* and *election.* Some are predestined to salvation by God's sovereign choice—and that is their only hope. For those who are not predestined to salvation—well, you know their fate.

Now here is a unique Wesley nuance: Wesley contended that the image of God in persons was not obliterated by the Fall; it was distorted, broken, obscured, crusted over with sin and self-will, but not obliterated. Sin was a malignant disease always portending death, apart from the miracle of God's grace.

Then came the second big difference. Wesley's understanding of "prevenient grace" and free will displaced the notion of election.

Calvin said, "We shall never be clearly convinced as we ought to be, that our salvation flows from the fountain of God's free mercy, till we are acquainted with his eternal election, which illustrates the grace of God by this comparison, that he adopts not all promiscuously to the hope of salvation, but gives to some what he refuses to others" (John Calvin, *Institutes of the Christian Religion,* II, iii, p. 3).

For Calvin, predestination meant that God has once-and-for-all determined, by immutable and eternal decree, all those who will be admitted to salvation and those who will be condemned to destruction. So, for him, justifying grace was restricted, limited, and particular. But not so with Wesley.

At the heart of Wesley's proclamation of the gospel was God's offer of grace to all. He felt the doctrine of predestination was full of blasphemy. "Of such blasphemy," he says in his *Notes on the New Testament* (p. 489), "as I should dread to mention, but that the honor of our gracious God and the cause of truth will not suffer me to be silent."

He argued on the basis of reason and experience, but primarily on the basis of scripture. How can it be?

This doctrine of predestination and election makes Jesus Christ a hypocrite, a deceiver of men, and a leader without honesty or ordinary sincerity. For it cannot be denied that Jesus everywhere speaks as if he is willing that all men should be saved. Listen to his pleas to the Jews in Matthew 23:37: "O Jerusalem, Jerusalem, killing the prophets and stoning those who are sent to you! How often would I have gathered your children together as a hen gathers her brood under her wings, and you would not!" His words are full of invitations to sinners: "Come to me, all who labor and are heavy laden, and I will give you rest" (Matt. 11:28). If you say that he did not intend to save all sinners, if you say he calls those that cannot come, then you represent the Son of God as mocking his helpless creatures by offering what he never intends to give. You describe him as saying one thing and meaning another; as pretending the love which he had not, "Him, in whose mouth was no guile," you make full deceit, void of common sincerity ("Sermon CXXVIII," Section 24).

Wesley was vehemently opposed to a doctrine of predestination and election because he felt it affected the whole of Christian belief and experience. The most obvious thing the doctrine of predestination does is to make preaching vain. Of what value is preaching to those who, with or without it, will be infallibly saved? And is preaching not a mockery to those who are not elected? They cannot understand or respond. To offer false hope to one who is damned already is a cruel charade.

But more than making preaching vain, the doctrine of predestination is, as Bishop Cannon reminds us,

. . . no doctrine of God, for it directly tends to destroy holiness, which is the end of all the ordinances of God. It takes away those first motives of holiness, which are the hope of future reward and the fear of punishment.

Immediately the Calvinist replies, "But man knows not whether he is assigned to life or death." Wesley answers that such knowledge is beside the point, and then makes this famous remark:

"If a sick man knows that he must unavoidably die, or unavoidably recover, though he knows not which, it is unreasonable for him to take any physic at all.

He might justly say (and so I have heard some speak, both in bodily sickness and spiritual) 'If I am ordained to life, I shall live; if to death, I shall die; so I need not trouble myself about it'" (Cannon, *The Theology of John Wesley,* p. 95).

Wesley argued that predestination tends to destroy the comforts of religion, as well as any zeal for good works. But Wesley's big claim was that predestination overthrows the whole Christian revelation of who God is as we see the Eternal in Jesus Christ. In his sometimes extreme way of putting things, Wesley said the doctrine pictures God as worse than the devil, more *false, cruel,* and *unjust.*

More *false;* because the devil, liar as he is, hath never said, "He willeth all men to be saved." More *unjust;* because the devil cannot, if he would, be guilty of such an injustice as you ascribe to God, when you say that God condemned millions of souls to everlasting fire, prepared for the devil and his angels, for continuing sin for want of that grace he *will not* give them, they cannot avoid. And more *cruel;* because that unhappy spirit "seeketh rest and findeth none;" so that his own restless misery is a kind of temptation to him to tempt others. But God resteth in his high and holy place; so that to suppose him, of his own mere motion, of his pure will and pleasure, happy as he is, to doom his creatures, whether they will or no, to endless misery, is to impute such cruelty to him as we cannot impute even to the great enemy of God and Man" (Sermon CXXVIII, Section 25).

If we had to select a single gospel message to present the essence of God's intention for us, would it not be that text from John 3:16-17? "For God so loved the world that he gave his only Son, so that everyone who believes in him may not perish but have eternal life. Indeed God did not send the Son into the world to condemn the world, but in order that the world might be saved through him." There's nothing exclusive or limited about that.

So, we United Methodists contend with John Wesley that sin is universal, but that grace is free in all and free for all, that whosoever will, may come.

## REGENERATION IS REQUIRED

Since sin is universal and is a malignant infection in our life, to use a medical image, radical surgery is essential to deal with it. *Regeneration* is required; a new birth. Not only are we forgiven, not only are we reconciled to God, we are made new, regenerated. This is what the psalmist was pleading for: "Create in me a clean heart, O God, and put a new and right spirit within me" (Psalm 51:10). This is what Paul contended would happen to us: "If any one is in Christ, there is a new creation; everything old has passed away; see, everything has become new!" (2 Cor. 5:17).

Now this requires radical surgery. And the radical surgery that will heal the malignant disease of sin involves a three-fold prescription: One, repentance which flows from honest self-knowledge and includes genuine sorrow and remorse; two, renunciation of self-will, a willingness to yield our wills to Christ since our will is the seat of our sin; and three, faith, which is a complete trust in God's sheer unmerited grace.

We are not helpless creatures, predistined to either eternal death or eternal life. We *are* free. We *do* participate in our salvation. We respond. When we finally come to ourselves and realize that we are sinners beyond hope of saving ourselves, that God's grace is for us, that God's unmerited love is not to be earned but to be received, we drop to our knees to receive our Redeemer in an embrace of faith and acceptance.

Here is a hint of it in the story of Benjamin West who tells us about how he became a painter. One day his mother went out, leaving him in charge of his little sister Sally. He discovered some bottles of colored ink and began to paint Sally's portrait. He really made a mess of things. Ink blots were all over. On her return, the mother saw the mess, but grace prevailed. She said nothing, picked up one piece of paper, and saw the drawing. "It's Sally," she said immediately and excitedly, and then gave Benjamin a kiss. Later, this great painter, Benjamin West, said, "My mother's kiss made me a painter."

God's kiss of grace makes us Christian—an extravagant grace that works within us, preveniently, preserving that last bit of freedom that is ours to respond to, working as unmerited love to justify us and account us as righteous even though we are sinners— to *regenerate us,* to give us new birth—and finally sanctify us, making us new creatures. It is sanctifying grace that we will discuss in the next chapter.

Wesley closed his sermon on original sin with this word:

Keep to the plain old faith, "once delivered to the saints," and delivered by the Spirit of God to our hearts. Know your disease! Know your cure! You were born to sin: therefore, "you must be born again," born of God. By nature ye are wholly corrupted: by grace ye shall be wholly renewed. In Adam, ye all died: in the second Adam, in Christ, ye all are made alive. "You that were dead in sins hath He quickened": he hath already given you a principle of life, even faith in Him who loved you and gave Himself for you! Now "go on from faith to faith," until your whole sickness be healed, and all that "mind be in you which was also in Christ Jesus"! (*Fifty-Three Sermons,* p. 566).

To that, I only add that redeemed by Christ, we will continue to sing in awe:

> And can it be that I should gain
> An interest in the Savior's blood!
> Died he for me? who caused his pain!
> For me? who him to death pursued?
> Amazing love! how can it be
> That thou, my God, shouldst die for me?
>                  (*The United Methodist Hymnal,* #363)

## QUESTIONS FOR PERSONAL REFLECTION

1. Augustine recognized his bent to sin in the relatively harmless incident of stealing pears (page 26). Looking back in your own life, is there an experience that witnesses to you the fact that *in each of us there is sin*?

2. Reflect on the fire that burns beneath the town of Centralia, Pennsylvania (page 27). Do you experience recurring breakouts of anger, greed, selfishness, possessiveness, lust, jealousy, etc., that remind you of sin in your life?

3. Look at the immediate past week of your life. Has anything happened to remind you of the residual presence of sin in your life?

4. Read Romans 7:18-24. After pondering Paul's description, write a paragraph about your own struggle with sin. Write enough to express your feelings as clearly as possible.

5. Recall the last conversation you had with anyone about sin. What did that conversation reflect about how seriously we take the problem of sin?

6. Look at your life over the past month. What do your actions, attitudes, and relationships say about the contention that *we are able to sin or not to sin as we choose?*

7. Wesley's understanding of prevenient grace and free will displaced the Calvinist notions of predestination and election (pages 29-30). Take some time to ponder this contrast. How does this challenge your thinking about God? About your relationship to God?

8. Read the paragraph on pages 31-32 that begins, "Now this requires radical surgery. . . ." How have you responded to this threefold prescription? What part of it may not have been completed in your life?

Write your own prayer to God in response to this prescription.

## QUESTIONS FOR GROUP SHARING

1. Invite two or three people to share their experiences in life that witness to the fact that *in each of us there is sin.*

2. Discuss why Wesley talked more about the *universality* of sin than about "original" sin (pages 26-27).

3. Reflecting on the image of the fire burning beneath Centralia, Pennsylvania, share other images or experiences in your own life which illustrate the universality, the residual presence, of sin.

4. Discuss the following two questions:

   Is there within our culture and in the church an assumption that the ills of humankind can be overcome with proper education, healthy environment, social caring about fundamental human needs, and political and social commitments to human good?

   What is the evidence in your community, and in our world, that this assumption about curing our human ills is true or false?

5. Discuss your personal beliefs and understandings, as well as what you have heard the church say, about sin as the source of human ills.

6. Look at the discussion you have just had in the light of Wesley's word that recognizing the reality of universal sin is "the first distinguishing point between heathenism and Christianity." (Read the entire statement on pages 28-29.)

7. Discuss the notion of predestination in terms of what it says about God's nature. Think about this in terms of God's *sovereignty,* the Calvinist's primary concern, and God's *universal grace and love,* the Wesleyan emphasis. How do we harmonize sovereignty and universal grace?

8. Ask if anyone would like to share her or his personal response to the threefold prescription for the healing of sin (no. 8 in "Questions for Personal Reflection").

# Chapter IV
# *But No One Can Be Perfect! Who Says?*

*For this is the will of God, your sanctification: that you abstain from fornication* (1 Thess. 4:3).

*For God did not call us to impurity, but in holiness* (1 Thess. 4:7).

*For I am the Lord who brought you up from the land of Egypt, to be your God; you shall be holy, for I am holy* (Lev. 11:45).

*Be perfect, therefore, as your heavenly Father is perfect* (Matt. 5:48).

*Let those of us then who are mature be of the same mind; and if you think differently about anything, this too God will reveal to you* (Phil. 3:15).

For me to write a chapter on Christian perfection may appear to those who know me like the man who proposed to write a book with the title, *Humility and How I Attained It*. Even so, it must be done, for Wesley viewed Christian perfection as the *grand despositum* of Methodism.

We are returning to pick up Wesley's theme of grace. In Chapter Two we discussed *prevenient* and *justifying* grace. Now to complete the trilogy: *sanctifying* grace. Our attention may be riveted on the theme by thinking about perfection, for that is what sanctifying grace is all about: Christian perfection. Thus the title of this chapter: "But No One Can Be Perfect! Who Says?"

Wesley believed that God had raised up the people called Methodists to keep asking the question "Who says?"—and to do this by claiming and proclaiming the scriptural call to holiness of heart and life.

We could have chosen any number of scripture passages to undergird this chapter, for the Bible is full of injunctions to perfection, to purity of heart and life—to holiness. God put the call clearly in Leviticus 11:45. And Jesus put it as clearly in his Sermon on the Mount. Wesley said it this way: "Ye know that the great end of religion is, to renew our hearts in the image of God, to repair this total loss of righteousness and true holiness which we sustained by the sin of our first parents" (*Fifty-Three Sermons*, "Original Sin," p. 565).

Interestingly, Wesley chose Philippians 3:12 for the text of his basic sermon on

Christian perfection. You remember this verse as Paul's word about his own life: "Not that I have already attained this or am already perfect" (RSV).

Now that may seem to be an argument against perfection, but in his introduction to the sermon, Wesley reminded his hearers and readers that immediately after Paul's disclaimer, he made a specific claim in verse 15: "Let us, therefore," he said, "as many as be perfect, be thus minded" (KJV). This seeming conflict in the claim of Paul is a clear call to seek understanding of what we mean when we talk about sanctification, holiness, or Christian perfection. All three words point to the same work of grace in our lives—sanctifying grace.

Let us then seek clarity about the meaning of sanctification, this central United Methodist doctrine. To do so, we must review a bit. To picture the idea of salvation, Wesley used the interesting image of a house. Repentance was the porch; justification was the entry-door; and all the rooms in the house were facets of our sanctification. It all begins with repentance—when we are convinced and convicted of our sins, are genuinely sorry, and accept by faith what God has done for us in Jesus Christ. When we respond in faith to God's grace, we are justified, made right with God, not because of our merit, but by divine grace. *Justification* is another word for pardon. So justification is what God does *for* us. And now the big issue, our focus: *Sanctification is what God does in us.* As Albert Outler would remind us: "In justification we *gain* God's favor; holy-living is the life-process in which we seek to *retain* it [that favor]" (*Theology in the Wesleyan Spirit,* p. 57).

It will help us to realize that salvation, then, is a process—a process that begins with justification but continues as we grow in grace toward sanctification, which is the goal of our salvation. Sanctifying grace is the work of Christ within us—Christ's spirit restoring the broken image, completing what was begun in justification.

A tragedy occurred in the Wesleyan tradition in the nineteenth century, moving this doctrine of sanctification from the mainstream into an eddy that has been stirred only now and then in the mainline Methodist movement. A revival of emphasis on holiness began to move through the church. As is so often the case, people began to preach a particularized experience as the norm. Doctrines were clearly and rigidly defined. A big segment of the church objected strenuously to particular ideas about holiness, and especially rejected a notion of "second blessing sanctification." At the risk of over-simplification, the doctrine of "second blessing sanctification" claimed that in a second experience of grace, like that operative in conversion or justification, a person might have his or her carnal nature eradicated so that one could live a sinless life. Unfortunately, for some the doctrine was "cast in concrete," rigidly and tenaciously presented as the standard for Christian living.

Just as tragic was the reaction of many who, failing to be able to harmonize the proclamation about perfection and holiness with experienced reality, threw the baby out with the bathwater. Rejecting an altogether too narrow definition and sanctification or holiness, and fleeing from an obvious stance of self-righteousness, they went to the opposite extreme and forgot sanctification altogether. For some time, little attention has been given to "holiness" within the mainstream of United Methodism.

Yet no reputable Wesleyan scholar denies that this was one of Wesley's foremost contributions to an understanding of the Christian gospel and the Christian way. So, let's take a solid look at it. To do so let's consider three points:

One, what Christian perfection is not.
Two, what Christian perfection is.
Three, what sanctifying grace does in our lives.

## PERFECTION IS NOT . . .

First, What Christian perfection is not.

*Christian perfection is not freedom from ignorance.* The Bible and Wesley are very clear about this: Sanctifying grace does not turn us into super-human robots, computerized and controlled by God to think and perform in all-knowing ways. No, we will always be limited in our wisdom and understanding. We will always "see through a glass darkly"—until that happy day in the kingdom when the scales will be removed from our eyes, and we will see clearly and know even as we are known.

If Christian perfection means that we will never in this life be free of ignorance and lack of understanding, it certainly follows that *we will neither be free of error or mistake*. John Wesley put a proviso on this one. He said, "It is true, the children of God do not mistake as to the things essential to salvation: they do not 'put darkness for light, or light for darkness': neither 'seek death in error of their life.' For they are 'taught of God'; and the way which he teaches them, the way of holiness, is so plain, that 'the wayfaring man, though a fool, need not err therein.' But in things unessential to salvation they do err, and that frequently" (Sermon XXXV, *Fifty-Three Sermons,* p. 510).

Wesley wanted to leave no excuse for the superficial notion that we do not know enough to be saved, or that we do not know enough to live a holy life.

I'm especially impressed by what Wesley said about interpretation of scripture, for this has been the cause for schism in the church throughout our history. Listen to him: "Nay, with regard to the holy Scriptures themselves, as careful as they are to avoid it, the best of men are liable to mistake, and do mistake day by day; especially with respect to those parts thereof which less immediately relate to practice. Hence, even the children of God are not agreed as to the interpretation of many places in holy writ; nor is there difference of opinion any proof that they are not the children of God, on either side; but it is proof that we are no more to expect any living man to be infallible, than to be omniscient" (Sermon XXV, Ibid., p. 511).

The third thing Christian perfection is not is *freedom from infirmities*. Again, we need to be clear about the meaning. By infirmities Wesley was not giving anyone an out to sin—in fact he warned against giving this "soft title to known sins." Let Wesley state his own conviction on this matter.

So, one man tells us, "Every man has his infirmity, and mine is drunkedness"; another has the infirmity of uncleanness; another, that of taking God's holy name in vain; and yet another has the infirmity of calling his brother, "Thou fool" or returning "railing for railing." It is plain that all you who thus speak, if ye repent not, shall, with your infirmities go quick to hell! But I mean hereby, not only those which are properly termed *bodily infirmities,* but all those inward or outward imperfections which are not of a moral nature (Sermon XXXV, Ibid., p. 511).

The last thing Christian perfection is not is *freedom from temptation.* "Such freedom from temptation belongeth not to this life." Wesley had a marvelous way of challenging complacency and shattering self-righteous images. In the matter of temptation he said of those who were satisfied with a form of godliness they were practicing: "There are also many whom the wise enemy of souls seeing to be fast asleep in the dead form of godliness, will not tempt to gross sin, lest they should awake before they drop into everlasting burnings" (Sermon XXV, Ibid., p. 512).

As he dealt with such self-righteous people harshly, he dealt with others tenderly:

I know there are also children of God who, being now justified freely, having found redemption in the blood of Christ, for the present feel no temptation. God hath said to their enemies, "Touch not Mine anointed, and to My children no harm." And for this season, it may be weeks or months. He causes them to ride on high places, He beareth them on eagles' wings, above all the fiery darts of the wicked one. But this state will not last always; as we may learn from that single consideration, that the Son of God Himself, in the days of His flesh, was tempted even to the end of His life (Sermon XXXV, Ibid., p. 512).

Let me reiterate. Christian perfection is not freedom or exemption from ignorance, mistakes, infirmities, or temptation.

## PERFECTION IS . . .

Now the second consideration: What Christian perfection is.

This requires looking at the whole picture of salvation as Wesley perceived it in scripture and experience.

Wesley placed a strong emphasis on regeneration or the new birth as distinguished from justification. Many Christian thinkers do not make this distinction, but Wesley had a clear picture of what he called the "way of salvation" in which he stated the difference.

He used the text from John 3:7, "You must be born anew," for his sermon on "The New Birth." He began that sermon saying,

> If any doctrines within the whole compass of Christianity may be properly termed "fundamental" they are doubtless these two—the doctrine of justification, and that of the new birth: the former relating to that great work which God does *for us*, in forgiving our sins; the latter, to the great work which God does *for* us, in renewing our fallen nature (*Fifty-Three Sermons*, p. 567).

Though distinctive, the doctrines of justification and new birth belong together. God acts for us to forgive us *and* begins the restoration of the divine image within us at the same time. This is the reason the new birth is such a powerful image. As our physical birth is the momentous beginning of our physical life on earth, our new life in Christ is the beginning of a life of our souls for spiritual growth. We are by God's grace redeemed from sin, justified in relation to him. We are also born of the Spirit.

Wesley defined the nature of the new birth in this fashion:

> It is that great change which God works in the soul when He brings it into life; when He raises it from the death of sin to the life of righteousness. It is the change wrought in the whole soul by the almighty Spirit of God when it is "created anew in Christ Jesus"; when it is "renewed after the image of God in righteousness and true holiness"; when the love of the world is changed into the love of God; pride into humility; passion into meekness; hatred, envy, malice, into a sincere, tender, disinterested love for all mankind (*Fifty-Three Sermons*, "The New Birth," p. 573).

In a word, it is that change whereby the earthly, sensual, devilish mind is turned into the "mind which was in Christ Jesus." This is the nature of the new birth: "so is every one that is born of the Spirit."

Now stay with me, I'm not being picky; this is crucial. There is a distinction between God's action *for* the sinner (pardon and justification) and God's action *in* the pardoned sinner's heart (restoration of the broken image and of the human power to avoid and resist intentional sin). Albert Outler puts it this way: "We have no part in our justification before God, save the passive act of accepting and trusting the merits of Christ. But we have a crucial part to play in the further business of 'growing up into Christ, into the stature of the perfect man'" (*Theology in the Wesleyan Spirit*, p. 58).

Now this is important to grasp, because here again I believe we witness the genius of John Wesley in bringing harmony to an understanding of the gospel. Let me illustrate, hopefully without being judgmental. Albert Outler reminds us that in a strict fundamentalist theology there is a preoccupation with the work of Christ for our salvation, and an unhealthy indifference to human responsibility in the struggle for God's justice in human society.

On the other hand, the stereotypical liberal has a well-defined social agenda, and is ardently committed to the kingdom issues of peace and justice. But unfortunately, there is little emphasis in the so-called liberal camp on the foundation on which the kingdom is established, that is, God's personal salvation in Jesus Christ. So Outler concludes:

> The liberal speaks easily of Christ as revealer and exempler but tends to stammer when pressed back toward any evangelical notions of mediatorial sacrifice. This is why neither fundamentalists nor liberals have a more than tenuous hold on the *full* Christian tradition, as we have seen Wesley trying to put it together and hold it together. Methodists, in his train, have a less than impressive record in doing this as well as he did (*Theology in the Wesleyan Spirit*, p. 58).

Is it clear? Wesley put equal emphasis on justification *and* regeneration or the new birth. Both are works of the grace of God in our lives. In justification we are pardoned and reconciled to God. In regeneration, the restoration of the image of God is begun. And that brings us to sanctification.

Sanctification is not to be confused with justification or the new birth. Justification and the new birth may be the miracle of a moment, but sanctification is the task of a lifetime. The dynamic process of sanctification is to work out in fact what is already true in principle. In *position,* in our relationship to God in Jesus Christ, we are new persons; that is justification and the new birth. Now our *condition,* the actual life that we live, must be brought into harmony with our new position. That is the process of sanctification.

Justification, the new birth, is the starting point of sanctification. "It is the gate to it, the entrance to it," Wesley said.

> When we are born again, then our sanctification, our reward and outward holiness begins; and thence forward we are, gradually to "grow up in Him who is our Head." This expression of the Apostle admirably illustrates the difference between one and the other, and further points out the exact analogy there is between natural and spiritual things. A child is born of a woman in a moment, or at least in a very short time: afterward he gradually and slowly grows, til he attains the stature of a man. In like manner, a child is born of God in a short time, if not in a moment. But it is by slow degrees that he afterward grows up to the measure to the full stature of Christ ("The New Birth," *Sermons,* Vol. 2, 240).

So what is sanctification? It is, in Paul's words, growing up into human maturity, "to the measure of the full stature of Christ" (Eph. 4:13). It is, again in Paul's words, "until Christ is formed in you" (Gal. 4:19). It is a total response to Jesus' call. "Take my yoke upon you and learn of me." It is Jesus' promise to abide in us if we will abide in him.

There are two phrases which I believe will help us most in understanding Christian perfection: *singleness of intention* and *perfection in love*. I heard of a young man who received a letter from his ex-fiancée which read as follows: "Dear John: Words cannot express the deep regret I feel at having broken our engagement. Will you take me back? Your absence leaves me empty and no one else will ever fill the void. Please forgive me and let us start again. I love you. I love you. I love you. Your adoring Sally. P.S. Congratulations on winning the Irish Sweepstakes."

I'd say her motives, intentions, and love were less than pure! The heart of Christian perfection is the will. Kierkegaard reminded us that "purity of heart is to will one thing."

But how can our intention be called *single* and our love called *perfect*, while at the same time we know that we are obviously flawed? Steve Harper has provided a very clear illustration from parenting which provides us with a clue.

When each of my own children were small, they had the bright idea to bring mommy some flowers. Never mind that they plucked the flowers from the bed mommy had worked hard to cultivate. Never mind that they might have even taken flowers from their neighbor's bed! Their one desire was to please mommy and to show their love for her. So, in they came with flowers, weeds, and dirt. With faces aglow, they exclaimed, "Mommy, we love you!"

What did mommy do? Did she throw the flowers away because they had clumps of weeds and grass clinging to them? Did she refuse to accept them because they were pulled from her bed and the bed of a neighbor? Of course not! She saw the deed through the eyes of love, took her nicest vase, and proudly displayed the flowers on the table. She accepted the act of love, even though she might follow it (at an appropriate time) with a lesson in flower-picking.

So it is with God. He accepts our intentions. He sees our motives. It has to be this way, for the light of his impeccable holiness even our best actions fall short. The Bible puts it this way: even our best actions look like filthy rags in comparison to God. We cannot hope to match him in actions, but we can be one with him in motive. Our controlling desire can be to do his will on earth as it is in heaven. God knows whether or not that is our intention, and when it is, he calls it "perfect" even though it comes packaged with some weeds and dirt (*John Wesley's Message for Today*, pp. 95-96).

## SANCTIFYING GRACE AT WORK

Now move to the final question. What does sanctifying grace do for us?

First, it gives us power over sin. Wesley was rooted in scripture here, especially in Paul. "Consider yourselves dead to sin and alive to God in Christ Jesus," Paul said in Romans 6:11. No longer are we to be "enslaved to sin," he contended in that same chapter to the Romans. Now settle this truth clearly in your mind. In any given situation, God's grace is more powerful than the lure of temptation. *Sanctifying grace gives us power over sin.*

Second, sanctifying grace *equips us for ministry.* To be holy is to be "set apart." One of the meanings of sanctification is to be consecrated for the services of God. In Leviticus God says, "For I am the Lord your God; sanctify yourselves therefore, and be holy, for I am holy" (Lev. 11:44).

The call to sanctification is a personal call to holiness, but it is also a social imperative. We will consider this more in the chapter on "Holiness of Heart and Life." I like the way someone introduced Mother Teresa: "She gave her life first to Christ, and then through Christ to her neighbor. That was the end of her biography, and the beginning of her life." Sanctifying grace equips us for ministry.

Finally, sanctifying grace provides us an *experience in which we can grow.* Sanctification is not static. When we talk about sanctification, we're not talking about "sinless perfection." Wesley himself did not use that phrase. Christians do not commit *willful* sins. If they do, they lose God's favor—we call that backsliding. The impulse and power of sin are not destroyed in justification or regeneration. Wesley would say they are suspended. Sin is *present,* but it does not *prevail* in our lives. So Charles Wesley would sing his prayer: "Take away our bent to sinning." This bent to sin, the possibility that is lurking there, must be dealt with by daily repentance, daily spiritual disciplines, daily renewals of faith, and daily exercises of love until we have singleness of motive and are perfected in love. So, we too sing:

> Finish, then, thy new creation;
> Pure and spotless let us be.
> Let us see thy great salvation
> Perfectly restored in thee:
> Changed from glory into glory,
> Till in heaven we take our place,
> Till we cast our crowns before thee,
> Lost in wonder, love, and praise.
> (*The United Methodist Hymnal,* #384)

So, that's the work of sanctifying grace. It gives us power over sin; it equips us for ministry; it gives us an experience in which we can grow.

There is a marvelous story out of the life of George Mathieson, one of the renowned preachers of Scotland in another generation, that gives us a "feel" for what sanctification means. When he came to one of the great Presbyterian churches in Edinburgh, there was a woman in the congregation who lived in filthy conditions in a cellar. After some months of Mathieson's ministry, it came time for Communion in the life of the church. In the Scottish Presbyterian tradition, elders call on members of the congregation to sign them up for communion. When the elder called at this woman's cellar with the card, he found her gone. After much effort, he traced her down, finally locating her in an attic room. She was very poor; there were no luxuries. But the attic was as light and airy and clean as the cellar had been dark and dismal and dirty.

"I see you've changed your house," the elder said to the woman. "Aye," she said, "I have. You canna hear George Mathieson preach and live in a cellar."

That's the picture. Sanctifying grace: "changed from glory into glory" till we know singleness of motive and perfection in love. "Changed from glory into glory till in heaven we take our place." The benediction of Paul is a blessing and a call to Christian perfection.

May the God of peace himself sanctify you entirely; and may your spirit and soul and body be kept sound and blameless at the coming of our Lord Jesus Christ. The one who calls you is faithful, and he will do this" (1 Thess. 5:23-24).

## QUESTIONS FOR PERSONAL REFLECTION

1. Can you recall when you first heard the word *sanctification*? When did you begin to think seriously about sanctification as a part of your personal Christian experience?

2. Look back over your life. Locate experiences or relationships involving preaching about perfection and sanctification or involving persons claiming the experience, that were negative to you—maybe turning you away from even considering the experience for yourself. Make some notes about these experiences and your feelings about them.

3. Wesley insisted that perfection was not freedom from temptation, though there were persons who were delivered from temptation "for a season" (page 40). Have you experienced periods in your life when you felt free, totally protected, from temptation? What was going on in your life at that time that might give you direction for living your life always? If you have not known such periods, can you think why this is the case? Take time to reflect and to write two or three paragraphs about this.

4. In the questions for Chapter Two, you were asked to recall and to reflect on your own experience of justification. Go back and read the notes you made in those reflections. Have you experienced anything that shows the distinction between justification and the new birth? Or, have you always thought of these as one and the same? Make some notes about your own experience.

5. Sanctifying grace gives us power over sin (pages 43-44). To what degree, and in what ways, have you experienced this power in your life?

6. Looking back over your spiritual life, describe any period that you might label a "backslidden state."

7. Sanctifying grace equips us for ministry (page 44). Have you ever thought of God's sanctifying grace in this way? Do you feel that God has specially equipped you for ministry? In what ways is this idea a growing process for you?

## QUESTIONS FOR GROUP SHARING

1. Invite two or three persons to share how they came to know about sanctification and to begin to take it seriously as part of their Christian experience.

2. Wesley insisted that perfection was *not* freedom from ignorance, error, or temptation (pages 39-40). Does this definition help in avoiding some of the "negative" images of perfection and sanctification that group members may have had? Why or why not?

3. Though perfecting grace does not free us from temptation, we can experience deliverance from temptation "for a season." Invite persons to share their experiences related to this Wesleyan insight, and discuss why some of us may never have known such freedom.

4. Albert Outler wrote (page 38), "In justification we *gain* God's favor; holy living is the life-process in which we seek to *retain* it [this favor]." In this light, discuss the relation between justification, new birth (regeneration), and sanctification. What connects these movements of grace? What makes them different? Why is it important to see not only the connection but also the difference?

5. Discuss how sin can be *present,* yet not *prevail,* in one's life.

6. Sanctifying grace equips us for ministry. Invite persons to share where they have seen this at work in their own lives. What does this insight suggest about a merely private view of sanctification as inward piety?

## Chapter V
# *Assurance: The Privilege of All Believers*

*There is therefore now no condemnation for those who are in Christ Jesus. For the law of the Spirit of life in Christ Jesus has set you free from the law of sin and death. For God has done what the law, weakened by the flesh, could not do: by sending his own Son in the likeness of sinful flesh, and to deal with sin, he condemned sin in the flesh, so that the just requirement of the law might be fulfilled in us, who walk not according to the flesh but according to the Spirit. For those who live according to the flesh set their minds on the things of the flesh, but those who live according to the Spirit set their minds on the things of the Spirit. . . . Anyone who does not have the Spirit of Christ does not belong to him. But if Christ is in you, though the body is dead because of sin, the Spirit is life because of righteousness. If the Spirit of him who raised Jesus from the dead dwells in you, he who raised Christ from the dead will give life to your mortal bodies also through his Spirit that dwells in you. So then, brothers and sisters, we are debtors, not to the flesh, to live according to the flesh—for if you live according to the flesh, you will die; but if by the Spirit you put to death the deeds of the body, you will live. For all who are led by the Spirit of God are children of God. For you did not receive a spirit of slavery to fall back into fear, but you have received a spirit of adoption. When we cry, "Abba! Father!" it is that very Spirit bearing witness with our spirit that we are children of God, and if children, then heirs, heirs of God and joint heirs with Christ—if, in fact, we suffer with him so that we may also be glorified with him* (Rom. 8:1-5, 9-17).

One of my favorite writers is Loren Eiseley. He is an anthropologist and naturalist who can blend scientific knowledge and imaginative vision. He records his findings with the perception of a painter, the words of a poet, and the heart of a prophet. Here is one of his powerful personal reflections.

The sound that awoke me was the outraged cries of the nestlings' parents, who flew helplessly in circles about the clearing. [A raven had raided their home to eat the babies.] The sleek black monster was indifferent to them. He gulped, whetted his beak on the dead branch a moment and sat still. Up to that point, the little tragedy had followed the usual pattern. But suddenly, out of all that area of woodland, a soft sound of complaint began to rise. Into the glade fluttered small birds of half a dozen varieties drawn by the anguished outcries of the tiny parents.

51

No one dared to attack the raven. But they cried there in some instinctive common misery, the bereaved and the unbereaved. The glade filled with their soft rustling and their cries. They fluttered as though to point their wings at the murderer. There was a dim intangible ethic he had violated, that they knew. He was a bird of death.

And he, the murderer, the black bird at the heart of life, sat on there, glistening in the common light, formidable, unmoving, unperturbed, untouchable.

The sighing died. It was then I saw the judgment. It was the judgment of life against death. I will never see it again so forcefully presented. I will never hear it again in notes so tragically prolonged. For in the midst of protest, they forgot the violence. There, in that clearing, the crystal note of a song sparrow lifted hesitantly in the hush. And finally, after painfully fluttering, another took the song, and then another, the song passing from one bird to another, doubtfully at first, as though some evil thing were being slowly forgotten. Till suddenly they took heart and sang from many throats joyously together as birds are known to sing. They sang because life is sweet and sunlight beautiful. They sang under the brooding shadow of the raven. In simple truth, they had forgotten the raven, for they were the singers of life, and not of death (*The Immense Journey,* pp. 174-175).

Now that's a lesson from nature about two Christian realities which were distinctively emphasized by John Wesley: *assurance,* which is the privilege of all believers, set in the grim reality of *sin,* which can and often does persist in the life of the believer.

Loren Eiseley's story is a bridge between our discussion of sanctification in the last chapter and our theme of assurance in this chapter. The birds "sang under the brooding shadow of the raven. In simple truth, they had forgotten the raven, for they were the singers of life and not of death." It is a revealing image of the style of a Christian. How beautifully and with what power did Paul express it in Romans 8. Focus again on his claims.

Verse 2: "For the law of the Spirit of life in Christ Jesus has set you free from the law of sin and death."

Verse 5: "For those who live according to the flesh set their minds on the things of the flesh, but those who live according to the Spirit set their minds on the things of the Spirit."

Verses 15-16: "For you did not receive a spirit of slavery to fall back into fear, but you have received a spirit of adoption. When we cry, 'Abba! Father!' it is that very spirit bearing witness with our spirit that we are children of God."

Now to be true to our situation, we have to admit one fallacy in the image. The birds may have forgotten the raven as they sang; the Christian sings, but does not forget the raven. *The presence of sin and evil is always an ominous awareness for the Christian. Sin abounds—but we sing—because grace does much more abound!*

So we must consider sin in the life of the believer, and then move on to talk about the song-inspiring gospel of assurance which is a central belief of Christians in the Wesleyan tradition.

## POWER OVER SIN

First, sin in the life of the believer. Does even the possibility of sin sound completely out of sync with the Wesleyan teaching on Christian perfection, reviewed in the last chapter? Well, it does, and that's the reason we must face it head on and talk about it.

We affirmed in the last chapter that one of Wesley's primary claims was that *sanctifying grace gives us power over sin*. Recall what we emphasized about that point. Paul said in Romans 6:11: "Consider yourselves dead to sin and alive to God in Christ Jesus." In the scripture quoted above, Paul contended that "the law of the spirit of life in Christ Jesus has set you free from the law of sin and death."

A saving perspective on these radical claims is gained when we ask the right question. Our usual response to the question as to whether a Christian sins is "Of course!" But the more important question is whether a Christian has to sin. The answer to that is a resounding no!

Here is the key: In any given situation, God's grace is more powerful than the lure of temptation. That's where we must begin. That's the bedrock truth, and it is the witness of scripture over and over again.

This is one of the strongest tenets in Wesley's theology: Regenerative and sanctifying grace keeps us so long as we keep it. In Romans 8, Paul uses the terms *flesh* and *Spirit* to designate the alternatives. In the preceding seventh chapter of Romans, he gives a classic witness of the conflict that may continue to rage in the life of the Christian: "For I do not do the good I want, but the evil that I do not want is what I do. . . . Wretched man that I am!"

In Galatians 5:17, Paul puts it this way: "For what the flesh desires is opposed to the Spirit, and what the Spirit desires is opposed to the flesh; for these are opposed to each other, to prevent you from doing what you want."

Paul writes to the believers in Corinth and addresses them as those "sanctified in Christ Jesus" (1 Cor. 1:2). Yet he says: "I could not speak to you as spiritual people, but rather as people of the flesh, as infants in Christ; . . . for you are still of the flesh" (1 Cor. 3:1, 3).

This Corinthian passage gives us a clear clue to understanding the fact that sin persists in the life of the believer. These Corinthians were brothers and sisters in Christ with Paul, yet he saw sin in their lives—envy and strife; but he did not see them as having lost their faith.

Paul saw those persons in Corinth as "babes" in Christ. Now we need not get tied up with how long we may remain "babes" in Christ. To some degree, we may all be always thus designated. But Paul and Wesley would not be cavalier about this. Sin, and our struggle against it, must always be seen as serious business. Wesley made the point clearly by asking the question: "But can Christ be in the same heart where sin is?" He responded: "Undoubtedly, He can; otherwise it never could be saved therefrom." Where the sickness is, there is the Physician,

> Carrying on His work within,
> Striving till He cast out sin.

> ("On Sin in Believers," Sermon XLVI)

"Christ indeed cannot *reign* where sin reigns; neither will He dwell where any sin is *allowed*. But He *is* and *dwells* in the heart of every believer, who is *fighting against* all sin; although it be not yet purified, according to the purification of the sanctuary" (*Fifty-Three Sermons*, p. 665).

So here is the truth in one sentence: "Sin *remains* but no longer *reigns* in the Christian." Get that! Sin remains but no longer reigns in the Christian. We need to note this particular Wesleyan position because it is the foundation for Wesley's conflict with those who believe in eternal security, or what some Christians today label the doctrine of "once saved, always saved."

Listen carefully to this succinct word of Wesley:

A man may be in God's favour though he feels sin; but not if he *yields* to it. *Having sin* does not forfeit the favor of God; *giving way* to sin does. Though the flesh in you "lusts against the Spirit," you may still be a child of God; but if you "walk after the flesh," you are a child of the devil. Now this doctrine does not encourage one to *obey* sin, but to resist it with all our might (*Fifty-Three Sermons*, pp. 671-72).

This is what separates a Methodist understanding from those who believe in eternal security. We believe that it is possible to return to sin in our lives to the point that we forfeit our salvation. This is not easy to do, according to Wesley, but it is possible.

Thus it is not a question of whether God is able to keep us from falling. Of course God is able! It is a matter of whether we are vigilant in responding to God's grace—whether we allow the Holy Spirit to sensitize our consciences, making us aware of the "new sins" that spring up in our lives, and the sinful abuses of innocent human aspirations. Being kept by God depends on whether we will listen to God's voice and not allow that divine love to grow cold within us.

Let us restate the case by coming at it from a different direction. There are two widely held notions about sin in the believer that are different from Wesley's. One thought is that, "Yes, sin continues in the life of the believer, but it is not possible for sin to separate a person eternally from God. One may *backslide*, but still be saved—

*if ever saved in the first place."* This "if ever saved in the first place" provides a common escape hatch: "Well, the person was never saved anyway!" How can we make that judgment?

The second thought is that sin is completely *eradicated* from the believer's life. The error in this position is that it treats sin as a "thing." For Wesley, sin was not *substantial,* but *relational.* The question is not one of the *removal* of sin from our lives, but of *reconciliation* with God which overcomes the estrangement of sin.

For Wesley, the new birth is the coming together again of a person and God. God's justifying grace makes this possible, and sanctifying grace is the continuation of the restorative process until we are so at one in relationship with God that our intentions are single—to do God's will; and our love is perfect—to love as Christ loves.

When we talk about sanctifying grace giving us power over sin—and what seems to be an opposite point, that there may be sin in the life of the believer—we must have a clear understanding of what we mean by sin. Wesley meant by sin "an actual, voluntary transgression of the law; . . . acknowledged to be such at the time it is transgressed" (*Fifty-Three Sermons,* p. 216). Wesley always left open the possibility of involuntary sin, which he felt did not bring God's condemnation. But to sin willfully in a continuous way certainly jeopardizes our salvation, for it separates us from God.

That case was clear for Wesley. We *may* "fall from grace" and forfeit our justification, but we don't *have* to. Whether we *can* or *can't* fall is not as important a question as whether we *do* or *don't.*

There are two major principles of which we must be aware. First, there is the principle of the abiding potential of evil within our lives—the old way of sin, which remains latent even in regenerate persons.

Second, there is the principle of our absolute dependency on God. Even after we have been converted, we can do no good by ourselves, but must rely completely on the Spirit of God which performs the good in us and through us.

We must give ourselves to moral and spiritual discipline. As Christians, we repent daily, and cast ourselves on God's grace. We grow in that grace and move from the threshold of faith—our justification by God—toward the fullness of grace, our sanctification. And all along that journey, we can be kept from falling from grace, kept from forfeiting our justification by the glorious assurance of our salvation.

Fanny Crosby wrote it, not Charles Wesley, but it's great Wesleyan theology:

> Blessed assurance, Jesus is mine!
> O what a foretaste of glory divine!
> Heir of salvation, purchase of God,
> Born of his Spirit, washed in his blood.
>
> (*The United Methodist Hymnal,* #369)

And the third verse of that hymn states it clearly:

> Perfect submission, all is at rest;
> I in my Savior am happy and blest. . . .

## WESLEY AT ALDERSGATE

That leads to the primary focus of this chapter: *assurance*. Wesley's favorite text for this, one of the central themes of his theology, was Romans 8:16: ". . . that very Spirit *himself* bearing witness with our spirit that we are children of God."

Early in his ministry, Wesley taught that there was no authentic salvation without assurance. By the mid-1740s he had modified his position, believing no longer that assurance was necessary for salvation, but that it was the "common privilege of all believers." Wesley testified to this change in an interesting letter to Melville Horne:

> When fifty years ago my brother Charles and I, in the simplicity of our hearts, told the good people of England that unless they *knew* their sins were forgiven, they were under the wrath and curse of God, I marvel, Melville, they did not stone us! (Southey, *Life of Wesley*, Vol. II, pp. 180f).

Here we must tell Wesley's story of his conversion at Aldersgate, May 24, 1738. We've waited until now to do so because the core of that conversion was the *gift of assurance*. Recall the bare outline of Wesley's life:

Wesley was a priest in the Church of England, a very religious person who, from earliest childhood, had been taught the doctrines of the church. His mother, Susanna, was an exceptional person. She had nineteen children, and all of the children who survived were given two hours of religious instruction by their mother each week. What a task, and what a commitment on the part of a mother!

Having been nurtured by his mother and his father, Samuel, who was a priest in the Church of England, John Wesley had a conversion experience in 1725 while a student at Oxford University. We're going to come back to that conversion later because it played a significant role in Wesley's life. There are few examples in history of a more disciplined religious person: rising at 4:00 in the morning to pray and to study; meeting with others who had joined him in what was called the Holy Club; visiting prisons; giving all his money to the poor except that which was absolutely necessary for his own living. He was almost neurotically preoccupied with the right use of his time.

He was a man *desperately* seeking salvation and an assurance of his salvation. He was tirelessly bent upon achieving that, and as a merciless taskmaster, drove himself in all the religious disciplines and services that could be imagined. He even came to America as a missionary to the Indians—serving for a time in Southern Georgia near Savannah. But all of that was a failure, and it seemed to Wesley that his whole life was doomed to failure.

On the ship coming to America, Wesley came in touch with some Moravians, and they influenced his life tremendously. A storm battered the ship to the point that even veteran seamen panicked. Everyone was terrified except the Moravians. They were calm and assured. They gathered together, prayed, and sang hymns, apparently oblivious to the storm. Wesley saw in them the peace that he desperately longed for, and he learned that they called inner peace "assurance."

In Georgia, he met a Moravian pastor, August Spangenburg, who made a tremendous impression on him. At their meeting, Spangenburg instantly pressed the question, "Have you the witness of the Spirit within yourself? Does the Spirit of God bear witness with your Spirit that you are a child of God?" Wesley was surprised and did not know what to answer.

Spangenburg then asked, "Do you know Jesus Christ?" After a pause, Wesley responded, "I know that he is the Savior of the world." "True," Spangenburg said, "but do you know that he has saved you?"

Wesley's reply was, "I hope he has died to save me," to which Spangenburg pressed, "Do you know yourself?"

Wesley responded, "I do," but later wrote in his journal, "I fear they were vain words." He knew he didn't have what the Moravians had—assurance, the witness of the Spirit.

He went home from Georgia downcast in mind, despondent in spirit, pierced in his heart with the futility of all his efforts and the emptiness of his soul.

After a short time back in England, he visited his brother Charles, who was sick in bed with pleurisy. Charles confided to him that in the crisis of the illness, when his life was in peril, he had experienced the assurance of God's love and felt that no matter what happened, everything was going to be all right. Charles was able to accept each day as a gift from God and to enjoy it.

John continued to struggle. He had labored as diligently as Charles had. He had worked for that assurance of God's love probably harder than anyone in all of England. And you can imagine that when he saw that Charles had received what he himself had so struggled for, he was profoundly discouraged.

It was in that despondent mood that he went to a prayer meeting on Aldersgate Street in London on May 24, 1738. A layperson read Luther's preface to the Epistle to the Romans, and something new happened in his own life:

I felt my heart strangely warmed. I felt I did trust in Christ, Christ alone, for my salvation; and an assurance was given me that he had taken away *my sins*, even *mine*, and saved *me* from the law of sin and death.

A friend, Mark Trotter, has imaginatively suggested that the experience of John and Charles Wesley, coupled with the memory of the Moravians' response to the storm at sea, was the inspiration for the first verse of Charles' hymn, "Jesus, Lover of My Soul."

> Jesus, lover of my soul,
> Let me to thy bosom fly,
> While the nearer waters roll,
> While the tempest still is high.
> Hide me, O my Savior, hide,
> Till the storm of life is past;
> Safe into the haven guide;
> O receive my soul at last.
>
> (*The United Methodist Hymnal, #*479)

## THE GIFT OF ASSURANCE

Aldersgate was the watershed. It transformed Wesley from a slave to a son. He *knew.* That's a key word: He *knew* that, in his words, "Christ had taken away my sins, even mine, and saved me from the law of sin and death."

In Paul's word, he did not receive the spirit of slavery to fall back into fear, but the spirit of sonship—the sonship that enables us to cry "Abba, Father."

Aldersgate was an evangelical conversion that resulted in assurance. In his book, *John Wesley: His Life and Theology,* Robert Tuttle has captured the essence of Wesley's witness about this experience. Writing in the first person for Wesley, he has him say:

To summarize, Aldersgate was indeed a watershed between law and grace. The experience of faith, love, and power, as well as assurance, is no small thing, but the sum total of my agonizing search for the life of God in the soul of man must be considered. Struggle alone never justified a man; but man is rarely justified without it. Man can never be saved by works; but he can never be saved without them either. I was determined not to substitute one extreme for the other. A measure of faith had left me blind to my own dependence upon self-righteousness. I was not to be saved *by* works but *for* works. The Aldersgate experience taught me that faith alone was the source of power. The experience of these last fifty years has proven this to be true without doubt.

Following Aldersgate I then had to pursue God as wholeheartedly by grace through faith as I had previously done by the law. I was a "brand plucked from the burning" and the intensity of my desire to serve God (since 1725) perhaps made Aldersgate inevitable.

"Unless the servants of God halt the way, they will receive the adoption of sons. They will receive the *faith* of the children of God, by His *revealing* His only begotten Son in their hearts." Yet I had to keep moving. Faith is a process. Had I stopped there the experience of Aldersgate would not have lasted through the night.

So, the Aldersgate experience was the difference not between saving faith and condemnation, the almost and the altogether Christian, but between servant and son (p. 200).

Now once the Spirit makes that witness to us, the witness of assurance can be continually verified. It can be verified in at least five ways:

One, we can simply remember that the goodness of God once shown to us in Christ is the goodness of God toward us for all time.

Two, we know that we have repented of our sins, and can continue to repent daily.

Three, we are aware of change in our lives—and the awareness of assurance grows within us as we see changes continually happening.

Four, assurance is ours if we are aware of a new character being produced in us—if the fruits of the Spirit are growing in our lives.

And five, we know assurance if we find joy in the service of God.

There are few experiences that can provide more power in our lives than to have assurance of our salvation. Think what it could do for any one of us:

Our timidity and uncertainty about witnessing would be dissolved. We would not be intimidated by those "buttonhole witnesses" who come on like gangbusters. We would know that tenderness, patience, and understanding are authentic testimonies, as well as words.

We would not get overwrought with our Christian friends who insist on future security, for we would be assured of our present relationship with Christ.

We would be joyous in our service for God, but not *driven* in our works or mistaken in the notion that our works would save us.

We would be delivered from frantic preoccupation with taking our spiritual temperature minute by minute, because we could relax in our trust of the Lord.

And all of that would help every one of us, wouldn't it? It certainly helped Wesley. On Thursday morning, May 25, the day after his conversion, he wrote,

The moment I awaked, "Jesus Master," was in my heart and in my mouth; and I found all my strength lay in keeping my eyes fixed upon him, and my soul waiting on him continually. Then at St. Paul's in the afternoon, I could taste the good word of God in the anthem which began, "My song shall be always of the loving kindness of the Lord: with my mouth will I ever be showing forth thy truth from one generation to another." Yet the enemy injected a fear, "If thou dost believe, why is there not a more sensible change?" I answered "That I know not. But this I know, I have now peace with God." And I sin not today, and Jesus my master has forbid me to take thought for the morrow.

"But is not any sort of fear," continued the tempter, "a proof that thou dost not believe?" I desired my master to answer for me, and opened his book upon those words of St. Paul, "Without were fightings, within were fears." Then, inferred I, well may fears be within me; but I must go on, and tread them under my feet (*Works,* Vol. I, p. 104).

That can be our experience, with the assurance given us that we are no longer slaves but children—and that we've not been given the spirit of fear, but the spirit of adoption, whereby we cry, "Abba, Father," We can keep singing the hymn that Charles wrote in celebration of his and his brother's conversion:

> Where shall my wondering soul begin?
> How shall I all to heaven aspire?
> A slave redeemed from death and sin,
> A brand plucked from eternal fire,
> How shall I equal triumphs raise,
> And sing my great deliverer's praise?
> (*The United Methodist Hymnal,* #342)

Two challenges now to keep assurance alive:

This day, and every day, rejoice in God's lovingkindness and in the salvation that is yours. This day, and every day, repent of every sin and renew your faith commitment to Jesus Christ. And the Holy Spirit will keep your heart and mind in the love of Christ Jesus our Lord.

## QUESTIONS FOR PERSONAL REFLECTION

1. Recall some experience in the past few months when God's grace was more powerful in your life than the lure of temptation. Be honest with yourself, and describe the experience here.

2. Now recall an experience at some time in your life when sin prevailed. You sinned and you knew it. Be equally honest in recording this experience.

3. What do these two experiences teach you about the statement: "Regenerative and sanctifying grace keeps us so long as we keep it" (page 53).

4. Look again at the experience you recorded in answer to question 2. At the time of that experience, did you *feel* sin? Did you *yield* to it? In light of your responses to these two questions, live for a few minutes with Wesley's statement that we may be in God's favor though we *feel* sin, but not if we *yield* to it (page 54).

5. Looking back over your spiritual history from the time you became self-consciously Christian, has there ever been a time when you were in danger of forfeiting your salvation by turning again to a life of sin and "falling from grace"? Describe that experience and its outcome here.

6. Reflecting on your own recent experience as a Christian, do you feel that you know what Wesley called "assurance" in your life? Write at least one paragraph on your experience as a Christian and your feelings about assurance.

7. Two challenges are given on page 60, which summarize how Christian assurance is kept alive. Are these challenges part of your daily experience? What connection would you draw between your answer to this question and your feelings about assurance?

## QUESTIONS FOR GROUP SHARING

1. Discuss the following two statements: "Regenerative and sanctifying grace keeps us so long as we keep it" (page 53). "God's grace is more powerful than the lure of temptation" (page 53).

2. Wesley said, "Christ indeed cannot reign where sin reigns; neither will He dwell where any sin is allowed. But He *is* and *dwells* in the heart of every believer, who is *fighting against* all sin; although it be not yet purified, according to the purification of the sanctuary" (page 54). Read this quote aloud to the group, and then discuss the following statement: "Sin *remains* but no longer *reigns* in the Christian."

3. Ask any who are willing to share their memories and feelings about a time in their lives when they may have forfeited their salvation by "falling from grace."

4. In the light of this personal sharing, discuss the meaning of "falling from grace" and "eternal security." (If no one has an experience to share, discuss the concepts anyway.)

5. In view of John Wesley's teaching, invite persons to share their personal experiences related to the witness and/or the struggle of assurance. (Keep urging one another to speak not just of intellectual beliefs, but of personal experiences.)

# Chapter VI
## *The Church: The Dwelling Place of Wonder*

*I have heard of your faith in the Lord Jesus and your love toward all the saints, and for this reason I do not cease to give thanks for you as I remember you in my prayers. I pray that the God of our Lord Jesus Christ, the Father of glory, may give you a spirit of wisdom and revelation as you come to know him, so that, with the eyes of your heart enlightened, you may know what is the hope to which he has called you, what are the riches of his glorious inheritance among the saints, and what is the immeasurable greatness of his power for us who believe, according to the working of his great power. God put this power to work in Christ when he raised him from the dead and seated him at his right hand in the heavenly places, far above all rule and authority and power and dominion, and above every name that is named, not only in this age but also in the age to come. And he has put all things under his feet and has made him the head over all things for the church, which is his body, the fullness of him who fills all in all* (Eph. 1:15-23).

Somewhere along the way—I think I got it from one of my heroes, Bishop Gerald Kennedy—I connected a drama critic's definition of the theater with an understanding of the church. "The theater," said the critic, "is the dwelling place of wonder." Isn't that marvelous? "The theater is the dwelling place of wonder." But it's really a better definition of the church than it is of the theater. Think about it.

### A DWELLING PLACE OF THE GOSPEL

Consider first that the church is *the dwelling place of wonder of the gospel.*

Wesley defined the visible church as a congregation of faithful people, "in which the pure Word of God is preached." For Wesley, "the scriptures are a complete rule of faith and practice; and they are clear in all necessary points" (*Letters,* vol. II, p. 325).

In his pamphlet entitled "The Character of Methodist," Wesley said:

As to all opinions which do not strike at the root of Christianity, we think and let think. So that whatsoever they are, whether right or wrong, there are no distinguishing marks of a Methodist (*The Works of John Wesley,* London: The Epworth Press, 1950 edition, p. 7).

One of the distinguishing characteristics of Methodism throughout its history is that it has been catholic (that is, inclusive) in its spirit. The United Methodist Church has been ecumenical and open to other denominations. An example of that is the fact that we do not require rebaptism when persons from other Christian denominations present themselves for membership. (We will explore this more fully in Chapter Eight.)

Now this does not mean that we are unconcerned about doctrine and theology. When people make a profession of faith and desire to be baptized, we ask these questions:

Do you renounce the spiritual forces of wickedness, reject the evil powers of this world, and repent of your sin?

Do you accept the freedom and power God gives you to resist evil, injustice, and oppression in whatever forms they present themselves?

Do you confess Jesus Christ as your Savior, put your whole trust in his grace, and promise to serve him as your Lord, in union with the church which Christ has opened to people of all ages, nations, and races?

Then, before the actual baptism with the laying on of hands, the pastor invites all present to profess the Christian faith as contained in the Old and New Testaments. This is carried out with another set of questions: Do you believe in God the Father? Do you believe in Jesus Christ? Do you believe in the Holy Spirit? And the people, including the candidate for baptism, respond in each case with appropriate expressions of classical Christian faith as contained in the Apostles' Creed.

We assume that a positive response to these questions is essential as a Christian affirmation of faith and for membership in the church. The church is the dwelling place of the wonder of the gospel, where the faith once delivered to the saints—the faith that has come to us primarily through scripture—is proclaimed, responded to, and lived out in the world.

For Wesley, Ephesians 4:1-6 was a controlling text for his understanding of the church. Here the unity of believers is emphasized, under the classic affirmation of our unity in "one Lord, one faith, one baptism" (Eph. 4:5). When Wesley talked about "one faith," he did not mean a single code of doctrine. He confessed his indebtedness to Roman Catholic, Lutheran, Reformed, Puritan, Anglican, and Orthodox traditions. "Right doctrine" was never a condition for membership in the Methodist Society, but "a desire to flee from the wrath to come"—i.e., a desire for salvation.

Even so, Wesley was not ambiguous about the "one faith" of the church. He tenaciously believed that the fundamental doctrines of Christianity were set forth in scripture. These doctrines had been articulated in the major creeds of the first 450 years of church history, and were described in the "Thirty-nine Articles of Religion" of the Anglican Church.

Wesley singles out three things that are essential to a visible church:

First: Living faith, without which, indeed, there can be no church at all, neither visible or invisible. Secondly: Preaching, and consequently hearing, the pure word of God, else that faith would languish and die. And, thirdly, a due administration of the Sacraments—the ordinary means whereby God increaseth faith (*Works,* Vol. VIII, 31).

So when we say that the church is the dwelling place of the gospel, we mean that here scripture is preeminent as the rule of faith and action, and that the real question of faith is not so much content, but, "How does faith operate in the church?" Thus the following affirmation of the church:

## A DWELLING PLACE OF CHRISTIAN FELLOWSHIP

*The church is the dwelling place of Christian fellowship.* Wesley had an exceedingly strong doctrine of the church. His commitment to the church was unquestioned. The fact that he remained a priest in the Church of England, that he resisted the idea of the Methodist movement becoming a denomination, and that he urged all the members of Methodist Societies to stay in communion with and receive the sacraments of the Anglican Church—all this and his total life demonstrated his love for and commitment to the established church.

Yet Wesley knew that it took more than hearing the Word and participating in the sacraments for Christian growth and discipleship. A deep fellowship for mutual encouragement, examination, accountability, and service was essential. Wesley talked about one loving heart setting another heart on fire. And that's a powerful image.

The fellowship for hearts setting each other on fire in the early Methodist movement was the class meeting. This was Wesley's effort to restore the depth and transforming power of the fellowship present in the early church. He felt the Church of England did not sufficiently provide for the fellowship of Christian people, which he sensed to have been the unique characteristic of the early church. Speaking of the failure of the fellowship in the church of England, he wrote,

Look east or west, north or south; name what parish you please: Is this Christian fellowship there? Rather, are not the bulk of parishioners a mere rope of sand? What Christian connection is there between them? What intercourse in spiritual things? What watching over each other's souls? What bearing of one another's burdens? (Colin Williams, *John Wesley's Theology Today,* p. 151).

So Wesley established class meetings to provide the fellowship of one loving heart setting another on fire. The class meetings were neither rivals to nor substitutes for the church in its ministry. They complemented the church by offering a more intense and personal encounter of faith and grace within a context of mutual accountability. It was the class meeting that conserved the results of revival preaching, and became the principal avenue of pastoral care during the Wesleyan revival.

In the class meeting five questions were asked:

1. What known sins have you committed since our last meeting?
2. What temptations have you met with?
3. How were you delivered?
4. What have you thought, said, or done, of which you doubt whether it be sin or not?
5. Have you nothing you desire to keep secret? (Albert C. Outler, editor, *John Wesley* [New York: Oxford University Press, 1964], pp. 180-181).

Now that's a rather tough agenda, isn't it? Most of us would resist it. But the point is that it worked. It started a fire burning in the hearts of people which set other hearts on fire. In fact, it started a revival fire in England and in the United States. It may well be that the precise agenda is not appropriate for us—though it may be. What is not only appropriate, but absolutely essential, is that the church provide the setting of fellowship where people care for and minister to each other. That's the fellowship in which one loving heart sets another on fire, and the church is to be the dwelling place of the wonder of Christian fellowship.

This is how Aristides described the Christians to the Roman Emperor Hadrian:

They love one another. They never fail to help widows; they save orphans from those who would hurt them. If they have something, they give freely to the man who has nothing; if they see a stranger, they take him home, and are happy, as though he were a real brother. They don't consider themselves brothers in the usual sense, but brothers instead through the spirit, in God (Jim Wallace, *Called to Conversion,* New York: Harper and Row, 1981).

## THE DWELLING PLACE OF CHRIST

The church is the dwelling place of Christ. Now that's a bold word, but the church is a bold dream of God. Go back to the scripture with which we began this chapter. When Jesus was raised from the dead, God:

. . . seated him at his right hand in the heavenly places, far above all rule and authority and power and dominion, and above every name that is named, not only in his age but also in the age to come. And he has put all things under his feet and has made him the head over all things for the church, which is his body, the fullness of him who fills all in all (Eph. 1:20-23).

In this particular passage, Paul tries to communicate the breadth of Christ's power. It is resurrection power—the power of God "accomplished in Christ when he raised him from the dead" (v. 20, RSV). It is ascension power—"and seated him at his right hand in the heavenly places" (v. 20). It is dominion power—"far above all rule and authority and power and dominion, . . . And he has put all things under his feet and has made him the head of all things for the church" (vv. 21-22). In these three phrases Paul pours out his surging soul as he seeks to do the impossible—to capture in words the immeasurable power and glory of God's work in Christ: resurrection, ascension, and dominion.

Ephesians has been called the "Epistle of the Ascension," and that it is, because here we meet the exalted power of Christ. In the modern church, we make too little of the ascension of Christ. How much thought do you yourself give it? Does the ascension explicitly impact your life? The early Christians were post-resurrection, post-ascension Christians. They knew the gospel story: a Jesus who was once a baby in his mother's arms—but not that now; a Jesus who was a carpenter, teacher, companion, and friend—but not that now; one whose healing love mercifully blessed all he touched, all he could see and hear and speak to—but he is not limited by time and space now; a self-giving Suffering Servant who hung on a cross, pouring out his life and love on our behalf—but he is not hanging there now. God raised him from the dead!

But more: This Jesus ascended, and the curtain went up on a new act in the drama. Pentecost has happened. The Spirit of this ascended One was poured out on his followers, and the church was born. The ascended One is "far above all rule and authority and power and dominion." His name is exalted "above every name that is named, not only in this age but also in the age to come." Everything has been put under his feet. He is the head, the authority. He has been given dominion. And the church is his Body—the fullness of him who fills all in all.

Do you stir with excitement as I do when you think of that? The church is the dwelling place of the wonder of Christ. We—the church—we are his Body!

For Wesley, the lordship of Christ was the Christian's greatest joy. To live under Christ's lordship provides the experience that Wesley described as "sitting in heavenly places with Christ." But this was no passive stance, no resting calmly in rapture and ease. Christ's lordship calls for disciplined obedience and attending upon the means of grace which we will discuss in Chapter Nine. Wesley called the church "a body of people united in the service of God."

What does it mean for us to be the Body of Christ? I can never forget how the late

Bishop Kenneth W. Copeland answered this question. To be the Body of Christ is to be his presence in and to the world. To be Christ to the world means that *we must see through the eyes of Christ*. And what does it mean to see through the eyes of Christ? Through Christ's eyes, there is no east or west, no black or white, no slave or free, no male or female. All are one in Christ. Through Christ's eyes every person is of worth and the church must respond in loving concern for all persons. We must not be selective in our outreach, seeking only those who are like us. In Christ's eyes, every person is a person for whom Christ died.

Not only must we see through Christ's eyes, *we must speak with the voice of Christ*. You remember what Jesus said when, on the sabbath day, he stood in the Nazareth synagogue and launched his public ministry. He read from Isaiah: "The spirit of the Lord is upon me because he has anointed me to bring good news to the poor. He has sent me to proclaim release to the captives and recovery of sight to the blind, to let the oppressed go free, to proclaim the year of the Lord's favor" (Luke 4:18-19). If the church is going to be the Body of Christ, we must have the voice of Christ.

And as the voice of Christ, we must fulfill in our world today this ancient prophecy which Jesus declared was fulfilled in him. We must speak with the voice of Christ to human beings in every situation and every condition. It's not a matter of a social gospel *or* a personal gospel. It's a matter of good news of Jesus Christ. War and peace, inflation and the national deficit, how the government spends the taxes we pay, where and how people live, abortion, pornography, ethnic relationships— whatever is of concern to human beings is a concern of the gospel. The gospel has something to say for our human plight, whether that plight involves our politics or our economics. You can't forbid the gospel going into any area of human life. No area is off-limits to Christ.

So the church must speak fearlessly and compassionately the words of God's good news to every person, wherever that person is.

Not only must the church see through the eyes of Christ and speak through the voice of Christ, *the church must heal with the hands of Christ*. The ministry of the church is the ministry of redemption and healing.

In his book, *Immortal Tidings and Mortal Hands,* Bishop Arthur J. Moore tells how the Old Testament phrase, the "excellency of Carmel" (Isa. 35:2, KJV), came to have deep religious meaning for him. At first it really meant nothing beyond its poetic grace. Then he happened to hear a famous archeologist lecture on the subject of Mt. Carmel. The archeologists said that, on this bald mountain, lovely flowers were found. there was no known explanation for their beauty among the blistered rocks. This was the "excellency of Carmel" for Bishop Moore, and so the good bishop drew this conclusion:

Then I began to understand something of the rich suggestiveness of this saying. Jesus came to give beauty for ashes, joy for mourning; to make an old world young again, and to work his ancient miracle of renewal and release in the lives of those who were helpless.

The church as Christ's Body continues this work of redemption and healing:

—Among the poor and the elderly;
—In the divisions that continue between races, rich and poor, male and female;
—Among those who are economically deprived and politically oppressed;
—Among those who have everything except what they need to make what they have worthwhile and meaningful;
—With the emotionally and mentally ravaged, those in the tenacious grip of alcohol and other drugs.

Finally, the church *breathes with Christ's spirit*. You see, we're not only a *human organization;* we're a *spiritual organism*. Our life is the life of Christ's spirit. His spirit gives us power. Here it is:

A young Christian, a singer, was imprisoned with thousands of others in the National Stadium in Santiago. As he stood among the frightened and demoralized prisoners, he began a solitary song in praise of his Lord. A guitar was passed to him and the Spirit began to blow. Soon thousands were singing with him. As usual, the authorities were threatened by the power of God's Spirit moving so freely and openly. So they seized the young man and took him away. When he returned, not only had his guitar been smashed, but he had no fingers. Horrified, his fellow prisoners drew back, but he walked into the empty space between them, lifted his bloody hands, and again began to sing with a glory on his face. Once more the Spirit began to move, the people took up the song, and predictably the guards moved in again. This time when he came back, he had no tongue. Many wept as they realized what had been done to him. Everyone was watching. For awhile he stood motionless. Some thought he was fainting. But then they realized that his graceful, silent swing was a dance. And soon they were all swaying silently with him, inspired by his glory, moved by his spirit. This time when the guards came, they thought they would end it all, and they shot him dead. But the spirit continued to blow (William Sloan Coffin, quoted by Don Shelby in his sermon, "Lord, You Can't Mean Hate," February 18, 1979).

And the Holy Spirit blows today . . .

—In the dynamic renewal of the church in Korea;
—In the courageous stand of the church against apartheid in South Africa;
—In the luminous life of Christians in Central and South America, in their witness on behalf of the poor;

—In our local communities of faith that continue to win people for Christ, that serve others in his name, and who preach the gospel clearly and with conviction.

The Spirit continues to blow through the church that is Christ's Body. And as the Spirit blows, the gates of hell cannot prevail against this church.

Does it make your heart happy? Do you feel the jubilant joy of it? Do you feel the pulsating power of it? We are the church. We belong to the Body of Christ. And as his Body we are the dwelling place of wonder!

## QUESTIONS FOR PERSONAL REFLECTION

1. What is your favorite definition of the church?

2. How is your definition of the church confirmed, challenged, or supplemented by the definitions we have looked at:

"the dwelling place of wonder" (page 65)

"a dwelling place of the gospel" (pages 65-67)

"a dwelling place of Christian fellowship" (pages 67-68)

"the dwelling place of Christ" (pages 68-70)

3. Look at the congregation in which you participate. Write some notes about how your congregation reflects Wesley's three essentials for the visible church (page 67).

living faith


preaching and hearing the Word of God


due administration of the sacraments

4. Recall your most meaningful experience when the church truly was either the *eyes*, the *voice*, or the *hands* of Christ *for* you. Describe that experience here.

5. Recall your most meaningful experience when you were the *eyes*, the *voice*, or the *hands* of Christ *to* another. Did you act alone, or were you part of a group? Make some notes about that experience here.

6. What could you do to make your own congregation more fully the Body of
   Christ?

## *QUESTIONS FOR GROUP SHARING*

1. Ask each person in the group to share a favorite definition of the church. List these definitions on a chalkboard or newsprint, or ask someone to write them down.

2. Discuss how these definitions are confirmed, supplemented, challenged, or enhanced by those given in the chapter—the church as the dwelling place of wonder, of the gospel, of fellowship, and of Christ.

3. Discuss the collective experience of your own congregation(s) in terms of:
    *a.* Wesley's three essentials of the visible church and/or
    *b.* The definition given of the church in the chapter as the dwelling place of the gospel, of fellowship, and of Christ.

   In what area(s) is your congregation the strongest? In what area(s) are you most in need of growth?

4. Share with each other what you could do—either as a group or as individuals—to strengthen your congregation as the dwelling place of the gospel, of fellowship, and of Christ.

5. Ask the members of the group to share their most meaningful experiences of the church as the *eyes,* the *voice,* and the *hands* of Christ *for* them.

6. Ask the members of the group to share their most meaningful experiences—acting alone or participating in a group—as the eyes, the voice, or the hands of Christ *to* someone else.

7. Share with each other the most important things going on in your lives that help you to be the Body of Christ.

# Chapter VII
## *Holiness of Heart and Life*

*But if you call yourself a Jew and rely on the law and boast of your relation to God and know his will and determine what is best because you are instructed in the law, and if you are sure that you are a guide to the blind, a light to those who are in darkness, a corrector of the foolish, a teacher of children, having in the law the embodiment of knowledge and truth, you, then, that teach others, will you not teach yourself? While you preach against stealing, do you steal? You that forbid adultery, do you commit adultery? You that abhor idols, do you rob temples? You that boast in the law, do you dishonor God by breaking the law? For, as it is written, "The name of God is blasphemed among Gentiles because of you." . . . For a person is not a real Jew who is one outwardly, nor is true circumcision something external and physical. Rather, a person is a Jew who is one inwardly, and real circumcision is a matter of the heart—it is spiritual and not literal. Such a person receives praise not from others but from God* (Rom. 2:17-24, 28-29).

A Stanford University psychologist, Dr. Festinger, has a theory he calls "cognitive dissonance." As strange and new as it may sound, it's very simple. It refers to my awareness of the big gap between my ideals and my actions, what I believe and what I do, my goals and my deeds. We all have that problem. Paul felt that his people, the Jews, faced the problem in a special way, though they didn't know it.

Circumcision was the identifying mark for the Jews. Paul challenged his fellow Jews and the meaning of circumcision, calling for a "circumcision of the heart." Paul affirmed the call of the Jews to be "God's own people." It was with the Jews that God had made a covenant to be a "chosen race." To them the law had been given. The Jews were proud of that and therein was a problem. In their pride, they became the victims of "cognitive dissonance." Now Paul didn't use that phrase because he was a student of Gamaliel, not of the Psychology Department at Stanford University. But he did address this "cognitive dissonance" of the Jews:

You, then, that teach others, will you not teach yourself? While you preach against stealing, do you steal? You that forbid adultery, do you commit adultery? You that abhor idols, do you rob temples? You that boast in the law, do you dishonor God by breaking the law? (Rom. 2:21-23).

Paul accused the Jews of failing to harmonize *identity and action, belief and practice.*

## CIRCUMCISION OF THE HEART

The core of this scripture passage from Romans 2 is "circumcision," and that is the image upon which we build this chapter—the call of Paul for a "circumcision of the heart."

The problem was that many Jews had allowed circumcision, that unique mark of identification as a covenant people, to become superficial and meaningless. "Circumcision indeed is of value if you obey the law; but if you break the law, your circumcision becomes uncircumcision" (Rom. 2:25).

Paul made his case more clearly:

For a person is not a real Jew who is one outwardly, nor is true circumcision something external and physical. Rather, a person is a Jew who is one inwardly and real circumcision is a matter of the heart—it is spiritual and not literal. Such a person receives praise not from others but from God (Rom. 2:28-29).

John Wesley used the verse, "Real circumcision is a matter of the heart, spiritual and not literal," as the text for his sermon, "Circumcision of the heart," preached at Oxford University on January 1, 1733. This is the only sermon Wesley preached before his conversion at Aldersgate in 1738 that he kept in its original form and used throughout his life in teaching Methodists. This consistency underscores a distinctively Wesleyan view of the Christian way: holiness of the heart and life, or personal and social holiness.

As mentioned in Chapter Five, in 1725 Wesley had had a conversion to the ideal of holy living. He never abandoned that ideal, though it was cast in a different framework after his Aldersgate conversion.

Between 1725 and his Aldersgate experience in 1738, he consistently misplaced holiness. He was driven by the idea that one must be holy in order to be justified. That was the futile process which drove Wesley to the deep despondency that eventually brought him to Aldersgate. One of the decisive shifts that came in his conversion at Aldersgate was a reversal of the order of salvation—justification preceded holiness, not vice versa.

There is a story, perhaps apocryphal, of Bishop J. Lloyd Decell, calling in a pastor who had been disappointed in his appointment. The bishop said, "My brother, I want you to know that this appointment has been sanctified by long hours of thought and prayer."

The man replied, "Bishop, that's the strangest Methodist theology I ever heard."

The bishop asked, "What do you mean?"

The fellow answered, "According to Methodist theology, a thing has to be justified before it can be sanctified" (Roy H. Short, *History of the Council of Bishops,* Abingdon, 1980, pp. 62-63).

The man was right—though his argument has nothing to do with how bishops make appointments, I'm sure. Justification precedes sanctification. Still, according to Wesley, Methodists "maintain with equal zeal and diligence, the doctrine of free, full, present justification, on the one hand, and of entire sanctification both of heart and life, on the other; being as tenacious of inward holiness as any Mystic, and of outward, as any Pharisee" (Sermon, "On God's Vineyard," *Works,* Vol. VII, p. 205).

A part of Wesley's genius was his ability to adapt and combine diverse elements into a synthesis, to bring harmony out of what on the surface was disparate. Howard Snyder clearly points this out:

> The Bible says salvation is all of grace, not of works. It also says we are able to work out our salvation, that faith without works is dead. Wesley's way out of this paradox was through Galatians 5:6—"faith working by love." This became a favorite passage and theme. True faith shed God's love abroad in the heart, which became the fountainhead of "all inward and outward holiness."
>
> Wesley's genius, under God, lay in developing and maintaining a synthesis in doctrine and practice that kept biblical paradoxes paired and powerful. He held together faith and works, doctrine and experience, the individual and the social, the concerns of time and eternity (Howard A. Snyder, *The Radical Wesley,* p. 143).

So is the synthesis of personal and social holiness, holiness of heart and life, which is the theme of this chapter.

## THE LOVE OF GOD AND NEIGHBOR

It is important to keep a perspective on at least a skeletal outline of Wesley's thought, especially about our need of salvation. Again, Snyder states it clearly:

> Wesley's starting point was not the decrees of God nor the logic required to solve theological paradoxes. Rather it was what Scripture affirms: God is sovereign; beside him there is no other god; all salvation depends on his initiative and working. But humans, even though sinful, still have a measure of freedom. And if they turn to God, they can be his co-workers in the concerns of the Kingdom.
>
> John Wesley stressed the image of God as well as the Word of God. Human creation in the divine image was fundamental for Wesley because it meant a deep, ineffacable similarity between the human spirit and the Spirit of God which even the tragic effects of the Fall could not destroy. Salvation was still possible. But

only by God's grace, because sin put men and women under such bondage that they could never freely turn to God.

Like Gregory of Nyssa and other early teachers of the Eastern Church, Wesley saw the *will* as essential to the image of God. God had given men and women a will, either to serve him or to rebel. Now, because of sin, the will was under bondage. People chose to do evil rather than good. Salvation therefore meant restoring the image of God and freeing the will to do God's will. By grace, men and women could will to serve God. Thus, the highest perfection in Christian experience is to serve God with the whole mind, heart and will. In a passage typical of many others, Wesley says that true Christianity is "the love of God in our neighbour; the image of God stamped on the heart; the life of God in the soul of man; the mind that was in Christ, enabling us to walk as Christ also walked (*Journal*, V, 284, in *The Radical Wesley*, p. 144).

For Wesley, it was a matter of the circumcision of the heart which issued in love of God and love of neighbor—holiness of heart and life.

It was captured clearly and succinctly at the formal establishment of Methodism in America at the 1784 Christmas Conference in Baltimore. The question was asked, "What can we rightly expect to be the task of Methodists in America?" The answer came clear and strong: "To reform a continent and spread scriptural holiness across the land." That's personal *and* social holiness.

But what does all this mean? Simply put, it means that we as Christians are to be holy as God is holy, that the church is to be that demonstration plot of holiness set down in an unholy world. Jesus said it means that we are to love God with all our heart, mind, soul, and strength, and our neighbor as ourselves. And Paul said it means that *faith* without *works* is dead, and *the work of faith is love*.

Mother Teresa of Calcutta is a luminous example of one who took God's call to holiness seriously. She said, "Our progress in holiness depends on God and ourselves—on God's grace and on our will to be holy" (quoted by Charles Colson in *Loving God*, p. 123).

And another modern person who took God's holiness seriously was Dag Hammarskjöld, who said, "The road to holiness necessarily passes through the world of action" (*Markings*, p. 122).

Wesley would affirm this commitment: "This is the sum of Christian perfection—loving God, and loving our neighbor—these contain the whole of Christian perfection!" (Quoted by Albert Outler, "Wilson Lectures," p. 16).

Wesley spoke of "inward holiness," that is love of God and the assurance of God's love for us. And he spoke of "outward holiness," that is, love of neighbor and deeds of kindness. He was fond of speaking of persons being "happy and holy." For him the two experiences were not opposites, but actually one reality. "Why are not you happy?" Wesley frequently asked. Then he would answer, "Other circumstances may concur, but the main reason is because you are not holy" (*Works*, IX, p. 325).

But never was it personal alone. In his extravagant way of stating things, he made clear the unity of faith and action. "Christianity is essentially a social religion," Wesley declared, "and to turn it into a solitary religion is indeed to destroy it" (*Works,* V, p. 296).

What I'd like us to do now is simply underscore the two separately—personal and social holiness—and then speak briefly about the church as the holy people who will be the primary witness of holiness of heart and life.

First, *personal holiness.* The New Testament refers to Christians as "saints" and those who are "being sanctified." Perhaps the clearest scriptural call is Romans 12:1-2:

I appeal to you therefore, brothers and sisters, by the mercies of God, to present your bodies as a living sacrifice, holy and acceptable to God, which is your spiritual worship. Do not be conformed to this world, but be transformed by the renewing of your minds, so that you may discern what is the will of God—what is good and acceptable and perfect.

In the chapter on sanctification, I quoted from 1 Thessalonians 4:3, 7: "For this is the will of God, your sanctification. . . . For God did not call us to impurity but in holiness." In talking about holiness to the Thessalonians, Paul spoke of their relationship to others: "Do not transgress or wrong your brothers and sisters," he said. That was a negative expression, but the positive, simple admonition is "Love one another." Here it is in a reporter's story of a nurse in the Veteran's Hospital in Coatsville, Pennsylvania.

It was lunch-time in the psychiatric ward of the Veteran's Administration Hospital here. Patients privileged to leave the wards had gone to the main dining room. For the sixty-or-so left in the wards of Building Four, there was a small dining room with food delivered from the central kitchen. Building Four had one nurse and two orderlies to get the seriously-mentally-ill patients through their meals. Six hands were simply not enough.

A toilet had overflowed, but the nurse could not find anyone to clean it up. She tried to do it herself while she kept an eye on five patients in wheelchairs, along with a dozen others milling in a hallway, each trying to get her attention. Three times in twenty minutes she had to rush by a patient curled in a corner before she had a moment to stop and gently urge him to his feet.

"Doesn't this ever depress you?" a visitor asked. "Not really," she replied with a smile. "If I ever begin to feel depressed, I remember that I may be the only person who cares what happens to these men. And then comes the strength and patience to keep going, to keep loving them."

The question is, do we do our jobs in holiness? But, more than that, do we live our whole lives loving one another? That's the key to personal holiness.

Chuck Colson has written an illuminating and challenging book entitled *Loving God*. It is primarily a book on personal and social holiness. In one chapter, "The Everyday Business of Holiness," he makes the case that holiness is loving and obeying God. He gives a series of personal vignettes that illustrate some telling truths about holiness. Those truths are:

One, holiness is obeying God—*loving one another as God loved us.*

Two, holiness is obeying God—*even when it is against our own interest.*

Three, holiness is obeying God—*sharing God's love, even when it is inconvenient.*

Four, holiness is obeying God—*finding ways to help those in need.*

That's a good witness in our own quest for holiness.

## SOCIAL HOLINESS

Now, consider specifically the wider arena—*social* holiness.

Wesley said, "The gospel of Christ knows no religion but social; no holiness but social." The social impact of the Wesleyan Revival, though sometimes exaggerated, is hardly measurable.

Marquis W. Childs and Douglas Cater conclude that "out of the light kindled by Wesley and the evangelical revival came the great drive for reform movements that had a direct and continuing relationship to the life of the past 100 years" (quoted by Lovett Weems in *The Gospel According to Wesley,* p. 38).

Kenneth E. Boulding asserted, "It was not the economists who liberated the slaves or who passed the Factory Acts, but the rash and ignorant Christians" (quoted by S. Paul Shilling, *Methodism and Society in Theological Prespective,* Abingdon Press, 1960, p. 64).

Wesley was at the heart of it. One of the last letters he wrote was to William Wilberforce, blessing him and urging him on in his anti-slavery fight in England. "Go on," he said, "in the name of God and in the power of his might, till even American slavery (the vilest that ever saw the sun) shall vanish away before it."

Wesley and the Methodist movement addressed several areas of concern: poverty, slavery, prisons, liquor, war, and education. It is not a matter of recent concern that United Methodists have a "social creed" that speaks to these same issues, as well as to others.

Our temptation when we consider social holiness is to address the obvious: issues such as pornography, abortion, and homosexuality. In our zealous reaction to these, we disregard other issues that are equally serious, though perhaps more subtle.

We spend a great deal of our righteous indignation and energy over issues such as "prayer in public schools." Let me share a personal witness. I spent ten years of my life at The Upper Room in a ministry focused on prayer. I'm committed to prayer. Yet, the issue of prayer in public schools is not as simple as many of our politicians—who want the vote of us evangelical Christians—would make it.

I am committed to prayer, but there is a difference between Christian prayer and other forms of prayer. I would have had real reservations about my children, when we lived in Southern California, being led in prayer by the young teacher who had just come back from her latest weekend with a popular Eastern guru from Tibet. Or, by the teacher—deeply religious, but not Christian—who had just finished a crash course in "How to Conduct a Seance," which for him was what prayer was all about.

Do you see the point I'm making? I do not want persons who are not Christian, some who may be explicitly non-Christian, modeling prayer for my children. I want to give other persons the same right also.

Christian prayer is an act of the people of God who are committed to God's sovereignty and holiness and to the saving grace of Jesus Christ. Any other prayer is what the prophets referred to as the "noise of solemn assemblies," and what Jesus referred to as "praying thus to ourselves." The reponsibility for teaching Christian prayer belongs not to the public schools but to the family and to the church.

Now return with me to my original point about our tendency to restrict our holy and righteous outrage against the obvious. The United Methodist Church is clear in its position on homosexuality. Within our Social Principles we read that all persons are entitled to have their human and civil rights insured, though we do not condone the practice of homosexuality and consider this practice incompatible with Christian teaching. That being clear, let me make my point without anyone mistaking my position, and the official positions of The United Methodist Church:

The scripture that people use most in the condemnation of homosexuality is the story of Sodom and Gomorrah. The usual reason given for the destruction of these cities was sexual immorality—and certainly that was a big part of it. Yet, when the prophet Ezekiel talked about it, he said: "This was the guilt of your sister Sodom: she and her daughters had pride, surfeit of food, and prosperous ease, but did not aid the poor and needy" (Ezek. 16:49).

The point is clear: In our passion to scrub America clean we often narrow the scope of Christian concern. And, by our silence on particular issues, we implicitly embrace those things not on our hit-list, or the hit-list of our favorite politician, thus aligning ourselves with the subtle sins of privilege, power, civil religion, and idolatrous nationalism.

Do we hear Ezekiel? Certainly social holiness has to do with pornography, abortion, and homosexuality—but it also has to do with people becoming calloused in "prosperous ease," taking no thought of aiding the poor and needy.

We're rightly upset as citizens, and especially as Christians, about the present economic situation of our nation—the staggering deficit that grows daily. Hopefully, we are learning that there are limits to what we once thought was the endless abundance of the American economy. Government deficits must be curbed, lest they continue to fuel inflation, which is morally indefensible and threatens the very fabric of our national life.

But let's keep perspective. If inflation is a moral issue, as we believe it to be, so too is society's concern or its unconcern for the poor, the disadvantaged, and the oppressed. We Christians know from the Old Testament prophets that Almighty God has a fearsome judgment of a people who would "sell the poor a pair of shoes." And we know from Jesus himself that our judgment will be based on how we respond to the "least of these."

Now we could spend pages asking questions about social holiness.

—What does social holiness have to do with a morally decadent society that no longer questions premarital and extramarital sex; that has trivialized marriage and brought about a cultural situation in which there are almost as many divorces as there are first-time marriages each year?

—What does social holiness have to do with a prison system that contributes to making a criminal society, rather than preventing crime and reforming offenders?

—What does social holiness have to do with a nuclear arms race that clouds the world with ominous fear and drains the financial resources of the major superpowers?

—What does social holiness have to do with housing patterns that have resegregated the public school system?

I can't answer the questions in specific terms. But the questions themselves call us to a commitment to holiness of heart and life. I ask these baffling questions to make one big point: The answers must be preceded by something far more crucial. That's what I want to address now.


### IN THE MEANTIME . . .


What can we rightly expect to be the task of United Methodists in America? To reform a continent and spread scriptural holiness across the land. What is required for such a mission? The circumcision of the heart which will identify us as those people who love and seek to obey God, and who are committed to the promise that the kingdom of this world will one day become the kingdom of Christ.

But in the meantime—ah, that's the point! In the meantime, what is to be our task?

Our first and primary task is to be faithful to Christ. We are called to be the church, to be the kind of community we need to be in order to be faithful to the Christian gospel—to be the church we talked about in the last chapter, *seeing* through the eyes of Christ, *speaking* with the voice of Christ, *healing* with the hands of Christ, and *breathing* with the Spirit of Christ.

Our first task, then, is not a political or social one, though it will certainly make an impact politically and socially. We are to *be* the church—to keep criticizing our message, ministry, and life together so that we become who God calls us to be, a people formed by the gospel.

Will Willimon has put the case in a puzzling way: "We best criticize the world by being the church." Then he builds his case:

Our social concern may appear ineffective to the world. Jesus himself appeared ineffective in the world. His power was the truth rather than worldly violence propping up falsehood.

Our aim is not effectiveness, but a prophetic demonstration that Jesus makes possible a new social order based not upon *what works* or competing self-interest, but upon his Lordship.

This is not a withdrawal from the world. It is a plea to confront the world on our own terms. The imperatives, "Come unto me," and "Do this in remembrance of me," theologically precede, "Go ye unto all the world."

In its very existence, the church serves the world, not by running errands, but by providing a light, that is, providing an imaginative alternative for society. The gospel call is an invitation to be a part of a people who are struggling to create those structures which the world can never achieve through governmental power and balanced self-interest. By its very existence the church is a paradigm for a society, a demonstration which the world considers impossible.

For instance, Christian charity will always be more radical than social legislation because the world can never serve the poorest and most powerless. The best it can do is to give the less powerful a little more power and call that justice. The world can never give dignity to the very young, the very old, the very retarded, the very sick. All it can do is dole out a few meager rights and call that compassion. For the poorest of the poor and the sickest of the sick, there must be hope that is not dependent upon public policy but upon the promise that God's love is stronger than death, and that nothing shall separate us from the love of God in Jesus Christ.

Only the church can be the communal source of that radical hope. We must care for the world by forming the church around this truth and no other (William H. Willimon, "In But Not of the World," *Circuit Rider,* November-December, 1982, pp. 8-9).

This does not mean that we do not labor diligently as Christians for justice and peace. It does not mean that we do not take seriously the political process and work for changed systems and structures, for legislation and political leaders who will serve the common good.

But it *does* mean that we will not put our hope in these. We do not place our trust in any political party, or persons, any economic or governmental promise or panacea.

*We perfect our lives in holiness.* We live together in the church as a people who have already tasted the kingdom. We demonstrate by who we are, what we say, and how we live that there is a kingdom reality that transcends all earthly systems and programs.

Jim Harnish, a preacher friend in Florida, shared a story about the power of a photograph, which says something about what the church should be. Yousaf Karsh was the photographer. Some of you may know his works—a Canadian photographer who has spent the past fifty years taking photographic portraits of the world's great people.

The only portrait Karsh ever took of a person's back was taken of Pablo Casals in a small French Abbey in 1954. Karsh writes that as he was setting up his equipment, Casals began playing Bach on his cello. Karsh was so enthralled by the music that he says he almost forgot why he was there. He took his portrait of Casals with the little bald-headed man bent over his cello, frozen in time against the plain stone wall of that chapel. Karsh said that he took it that way to capture the loneliness of the truly great artists and the loneliness of the exile.

Years later, when the portrait was on exhibit in the Museum of Fine Arts in Boston, another old, bald-headed man came day after day and stood for long moments at a time in front of the portrait. The Curator of the Museum noticed him, and when his curiosity got the best of him, went over, tapped the man on the shoulder and asked why he stood so long before the picture. The old man, with obvious irritation, turned on the curator and said, "Hush, young man! Can't you see I'm listening to the music!"

Karsh watched Casals play his cello and presented a picture. The old man, looking at that picture could hear the music.

The church ought to be God's music—a picture to the world of what God wants the world to be. And when we are that, we will provide the radical hope all humanity needs. Our music will then permeate the whole of life, and we will hasten the day when the kingdoms of this world will become the kingdom of our Lord and Christ, who will reign forever and ever.

## QUESTIONS FOR PERSONAL REFLECTION

1. In your own spiritual pilgrimage, have you been conscious of any tension between experiencing "salvation by grace through faith alone," and the call to "work out your salvation in fear and trembling"? Describe your own experience in this regard.

2. Do you ever recognize a tension between your *will* and the mind of Christ working in you? If so, make some notes about this tension—how it feels and how it expresses itself in your life.

3. Looking back over your Christian journey, which have you paid more attention to—personal or social holiness? Why do you think this is so?

To which are you paying more attention now? Are you changing in any way in this regard?

4. Recall and describe some occasion or circumstance when you obeyed God though it was against your interest.

5. Have you ever been involved with a group in a struggle over a particular issue in which you fought for social holiness? Name that issue, and describe why you think the goal of holiness is connected to it.

If you have never been involved in such a struggle, why has this been the case? How would you explain your lack of involvement in the light of the call to "social holiness"?

## QUESTIONS FOR GROUP SHARING

1. Invite persons in the group to share any *new* thought or idea that came from the study of this chapter.

2. With what issue or idea did participants have the most difficulty?

3. Ask each person to share *briefly* his or her personal Christian journey with respect to personal and social holiness. Where has the emphasis been? Are things changing in any way?

4. On page 83 is Chuck Colson's definition of holiness as obeying God: Loving one another as God loves us; obeying even when it is against our own interest; sharing God's love, even when it is inconvenient; and finding ways to help those in need. Ask the group to share experiences of obeying God in any of these categories.

5. On page 84, we mentioned the issue of homosexuality and saw how the prophet Ezekiel expressed equal concern over some other less "sensational" social sins, for example, extravagant eating habits and failure to aid the poor and needy. In your opinion, what are the crucial social issues in your community that you and your congregation must address? List these, but give special attention to the "non-glaring" issues.

6. What would it mean, and what would have to happen, for your congregation to be a demonstration plot of holiness set down in an unholy world? Name two or more specific steps that would strengthen your congregation's witness in this area.

7. In light of all that you have discussed, invite the group to devise a three- or four-sentence definition of the "circumcision of the heart." Encourage the group to write this down in their study books.

# Chapter VIII
## *Style: Some Distinctive Marks of a United Methodist*

*For freedom Christ has set us free. Stand firm, therefore and do not submit again to a yoke of slavery. Listen! I, Paul, am telling you that if you let yourself be circumcised, Christ will be of no benefit to you. Once again I testify to every man who lets himself be circumcised that he is obliged to obey the entire law. You who want to be justified by the law have cut yourselves off from Christ; you have fallen away from grace. For through the Spirit, by faith, we eagerly wait for the hope of righteousness. For in Christ Jesus neither circumcision not uncircumcision counts for anything; the only thing that counts for anything; the only thing that counts is faith working through love. You were running well; who prevented you from obeying the truth? Such persuasion does not come from the one who calls you. A little yeast leavens the whole batch of dough* (Gal. 5:1-9).

Circumstances sometimes call us to do strange things—things we would not otherwise do. Circumstances also cause us to do things we should have done but never got around to before.

Two out-of-town visitors were walking along a street in New York City late one night. One of the pair, wary of the reputation of city streets at night, kept glancing over his shoulder, nervously eyeing every alley and shadowed doorway. Sure enough, his anticipation was rewarded. As the two rounded the next corner, two muggers appeared out of the darkness and closed in. The nervous fellow knew what was going to happen. He reached for his wallet, pulled out of a $50 bill and handed it to his friend: "Joe, here's that $50 I've been owing you for six months."

According to some critics, John Wesley never had an original idea in his life. He just borrowed from others. But the point is, whatever Wesley borrowed, he paid back tenfold and more. Even if it's true that Wesley only borrowed from others, that would hardly solve the riddle of this man and the spiritual dynamic of the Methodist movement. Wesley's genius and originality lay precisely in his borrowing, adapting, and combining diverse elements into a synthesis more dynamic than the sum of its parts.

Wesley also had the genius of putting an expansive, explosive truth in a single, sometimes simple sentence or a pithy phrase. He encapsulated his vision of mission and ministry in the sentence that has been on the lips of Methodists ever since: "The world is my parish." He borrowed from Paul to summarize his theology succinctly:

"Faith working through love." He gave a challenging and rather complete principle of stewardship in the crisp triplet: "Gain all you can, save all you can, and give all you can."

He put controversy into perspective, and defined what should be the position of every Christian in one terse line: "In essentials, unity; in non-essentials, liberty; in all things, charity." He described his whole approach to differences in belief and church order in the one question: "Is thine heart right, as my heart is with thy heart? . . . If it be, give me thine hand."

In this chapter, we will look at the *style* of a United Methodist. Style can be as important as content. There is a sense in which the "medium is the message."

Diana Vreeland, the undisputed leader in fashion, wrote her autobiography with the simple but *stylish* title, *DV*. It recorded her lifetime of living with inimitable style. She made a big point about the importance of style by referring to Japan. "God was fair to the Japanese," she said. "He gave them no oil, no coal, no diamonds, no gold, no material resources—nothing! Nothing comes from the island that you can sustain a civilization on. All God gave the Japanese was a sense of style" (*House and Garden,* April 1984, p. 36, excerpts from *DV*). It was the ultimate compliment to the Japanese from this fashion stylesetter.

United Methodists have a style that, to a marked degree, defines our uniqueness. As we look at some distinctive ingredients that make up that style, hold in your mind the fact that these marks are to be seen in the context of all the essential things we've been talking about in the preceding chapter.

## A CATHOLIC SPIRIT

First, a catholic spirit. This is a celebrated aspect of our style. This spirit is desperately needed in our day, because too many Christians are plagued with *xenophobia*.

You didn't know the church was plagued with xenophobia, did you? It's not a common word in our vocabulary. I thought about it recently when I saw a TV special on all the phobias psychologists and psychiatrists are helping people deal with.

A phobia is an exaggerated and persistent aversion to or dread and fear of something. Common ones that psychologists deal most frequent with are *acrophobia,* the fear of high places; *claustrophobia,* the fear of closed-in places; *demophobia,* the fear of crowds; *autophobia,* the fear of self or being alone; and *mysophobia,* the fear of contamination. And there are numerous others which are the source of great emotional problems. I learned a new one recently—*gamophobia,* the fear of marriage.

But back to xenophobia. Xenophobia is a "hatred or distrust of foreigners or strangers." Practically speaking, it is a fear of that which is different from yourself, the fear and suspicion of differences. It has been the phobia of people from the beginning, and still is. Xenophobia has plagued the church.

Peter and the Jerusalem apostles feared Paul and his work among the Gentiles. They were suspicious because they did not understand. That spirit within the church has often hindered the ministry of Christ. We fear opinions, positions, attitudes, and beliefs that do not match our own.

Over against xenophobia I want to put those celebrated words of John Wesley. "Is thine heart right, as my heart is with thy heart? . . . If it be, give me thine hand." Now those words are actually from 2 Kings 10:15. Wesley used them as the text for one of the noblest sermons he ever preached, his sermon on the "Catholic Spirit." it was one of the few instances in Wesley's preaching when the scriptural setting of the text had nothing to do with the sermon. Unlike most of us preachers, Wesley didn't take a text and depart from it; he stayed with it. Not so in this instance.

When Wesley sent a copy of the sermon to the Reverend Mr. Clark of Hollymount, that gentleman's criticism was, "Your propositions and observations have no more foundation in the text than in the first chapter of Genesis." That criticism was justified. Wesley took the words completely out of their grisly context in 2 Kings 10 and asked, not what they meant there, but what a follower of Christ should find in them. And from that exploration, he gave us a great word to guide us as we think about the catholic spirit.

Now, two points about the catholic spirit that are so important as principles in the Methodist style:

First, one of the real confusions within The United Methodist Church today is a misunderstanding and a misapplication of Wesley's concept of the catholic spirit. We interpret that to mean "theological pluralism," and such a pluralism is projected as both acceptable and desirable of what it means to be a Christian within the Methodist tradition. Taken to an extreme there is a fallacy in this concept. The way it is projected suggests that a United Methodist Christian can believe almost anything about God, Jesus Christ, and the essential doctrines that relate to salvation. But this is a perversion of Wesley's idea of the catholic spirit.

Such an uncritical, undemanding, unexamined emphasis on so-called pluralism was the furthest thing from Wesley's thinking. He was unreserved in his condemnation of what he called "speculative latitudinarianism," which would be his word for the way many interpret pluralism today.

From Wesley we learn:

A catholic spirit is not *speculative* latitudinarianism. It is not an indifference to all opinions: this is the spawn of hell, not the offspring of heaven. This unsettledness of thought, this being "driven to and fro and tossed about with every wind of doctrine" is a great curse, not a blessing; an irreconcilable enemy, not a friend, to true catholicism. A man of a truly catholic spirit has not now his religion to seek. He is fixed as the sun in his judgment concerning the main branches of Christian doctrine. It is true, he is always ready to hear and weigh whatsoever can be offered against his principles; but as this does not show any wavering in his own mind, so neither does it occasion any. He does not halt between two opinions, nor vainly endeavor to blend them into one. Observe this, you who know not what spirit ye are of: who call yourselves men of the catholic spirit, only because you are of a muddy understanding; because your mind is all in a mist; because you have no settled, consistent principles, but are for jumbling all opinions together. Be convinced, that you have quite missed your way; you know not where you are. You think you are got into the very spirit of Christ when, in truth, you are nearer the spirit of Antichrist. Go, first, and learn the first elements of the gospel of Christ, and then shall you learn to be of a truly catholic spirit (*Fifty-Three Sermons,* "Catholic Spirit," p. 502).

So then, the second point: Nothing is more needed in the church today, especially in the United States, than a catholic spirit. In his pamphlet entitled, "The Character of a Methodist," Wesley said: "As to all opinions which do not strike at the root of Christianity, we think and let think. So that whatsoever they are, whether right or wrong, they are no distinguishing marks of a Methodist." Remember now, Wesley is talking about things that do not strike at the root of Christianity.

—Does our mode of baptisms—*how* we baptize—strike at the root of Christianity?
—Does whether or not we have musical instruments in the church make any difference as far as real Christianity is concerned?
—*How* we serve communion—is that a grave issue as far as the faith is concerned?
—Is any argument about the millenium essential to the faith?
—Does it help to get all bogged down in trying to figure out when the Lord is going to come again? Is that kind of argument really a positive contribution to the kingdom?

Most of the things we get all stirred up about, that drive us to anger, and even divide us as Christians—most of that, I think, the Lord cares little about.

Remember what Jesus said to those Pharisees who condemned him for plucking corn on the sabbath in order that his disciples might eat? "The sabbath was made for man, not man for the sabbath." This is what Paul was saying in Galatians 5:1: "For freedom Christ has set us free. Stand firm therefore, and do not submit again to a yoke of slavery." And how gloriously and with what power did he write, "For in Christ Jesus neither circumcision nor uncircumcision is of any avail, but faith working through love" (v. 6).

This is what Wesley was getting at when he continued to admonish his Methodist flock:

I beseech you brethren, by the mercies of God, that we be in no wise divided among ourselves. Is thy heart right, as my heart is right with thine? I ask no further question. If it be, give me thy hand. For opinions, or terms, let us not destroy the work of God. Dost thou love and serve God? It is enough. I give thee the right hand of fellowship (*Works of John Wesley,* London: The Epworth Press, 1950 edition, pp. 7-15).

We need that as United Methodists. The world needs it—the catholic spirit lived out in our different denominations.

## HEARTFELT RELIGION

Now the second ingredient of a United Methodist style is what we often call "heartfelt religion." In Methodist language, this is the experience of the "warm heart." This has meaning at two points: the individual; and the fellowship, the larger group.

The Methodist movement was born in England and soon began to burn with a fire of love across the land, in large part, because of two big problems in the Established Church. One was *spiritual apathy.* Deism had flavored the intellectual and religious climate. God had become a benevolent ruler of the universe, removed from personal experience. In the arrogant rationalism that pervaded the day, everything had to be utterly reasonable.

The second thing that had happened was that the nature of the church as an organization had become *remote*, removed from life, not touching the people where they were. One cleric, for instance, had been made a bishop and given a lifetime stipend, but never set foot in the diocese over which he presumably had spiritual and temporal oversight. It was obviously all temporal and nothing spiritual.

Into that setting with those two characteristics—spiritual apathy and a remote church structure—came the Methodist revival with an answer to these two glaring, devastating failures of the church.

For spiritual apathy, there was the experience of the warm heart. People wanted desperately not only to hear the gospel, but also to experience it. So Aldersgate became the model: "I felt my heart strangely warmed, I felt I did trust Christ, Christ alone for salvation; and an assurance was given me that he had taken away my sins, even mine, and saved me from the law of sin and death." That experience was repeated over and over.

Furthermore, for people who experienced a church that had become lifelessly formal at best, and coldly remote at worst, the Methodists came with ministries of care and warm concern. The class meetings and bands of the Methodist societies became the settings for these expressions of compassion. People cared for and looked after each other's souls. Loving hearts set other hearts on fire.

When Wesley spoke of "social holiness" and "social Christianity," he was point-ing to New Testament *koinonia*. Christian fellowship meant, not merely corporate worship, but watching over one another in love, advising, exhorting, admonishing and praying with the brothers and sisters. "This, and this alone, is Christian fellowship," he said. And this is what Methodism promoted: "We introduced Christian fellowship where it was utterly destroyed," said Wesley. And the fruits of it have been peace, joy, love, and zeal for good work and work (Snyder, *The Radical Wesley,* p. 148).

One question we need to ask is whether this style of the warm heart is pronounced enough in our congregations, and in ourselves. And a second question: Are we providing the structures of care where persons can grow in grace and discipleship, where the fruits of the spirit can be cultivated?

These are the questions Paul addressed: "For in Christ Jesus neither circumcision nor uncircumcision counts for anything; the only thing that counts is faith working through love. You were running well; who prevented you from obeying the truth?" (Ga. 5:6-7).

In a lecture at Emory University, Dr. Theodore Runyon introduced what to me was a whole new way of thinking about the "heart strangely warmed" and structures of care as means for our growth in Christ and our life in the world. It is a new way of thinking about a Methodist style. He used three terms to make an important distinction: *orthodoxy, orthopraxis,* and *orthopathy.* The first two terms were famil-iar; not the third. Orthodoxy is right doctrine, right opinion, right belief. But Methodists have never believed that orthodoxy was enough. God demands right action, right practice, right behavior—that is *orthopraxis.*

Wesley recognized that many who can only inadequately formulate their faith, nevertheless, live transformed lives in constant fellowship with God (*Wesley's Works,* Vol. V, p. 354): "I believe the merciful God regards the lives and tempers of men more than their ideas. I believe he respects the goodness of heart, rather than the clearness of head; and that if the heart of man be filled (by the grace of God, the power of his Spirit) with the humble, gentle, patient love of God and man, God will not cast him into everlasting fire . . . because his ideas are not clear, or because his conceptions are confused." Wesley concludes, "I admit that 'without holiness no man shall see the Lord.' But I dare not add, 'or without clear ideas.'" This seems to place Wesley solidly on the side of orthopraxis and against dead orthodoxy.

In another sermon, he lists all the arguments given against aid to the poor, including the argument that most of the poor are not Christians but obstinate sinners. Wesley's rejoinder is, "Whether [the poor] will be finally lost or saved, you are expressly commanded to feed the hungry and clothe the naked. If you can, and do not, whatever becomes of them, you shall go away into everlasting fire."

Even with that kind of plea for *orthopraxis,* working faith, he always insisted that as faith without works is dead, works without faith profiteth nothing; that "all morality, all justice, mercy and truth—without faith—is of no value in the sight of God."

Neither orthodoxy nor orthopraxis alone is sufficient. And what Runyon adds is that even together, they are not enough. There must be *orthopathy.* This means right passions, senses, tempers, dispositions; and in the larger sense, *right experience.* This, says Runyon, is the challenge to a theology of conversion—

To recognize the crying need of humankind to be encountered and transformed by Christian faith in all aspects of their being, including the emotions, feelings, and experiences. Nothing less is a sign of the kingdom and its power in the midst of the present age. And nothing less than this kind of theology and experience ought to undergird our preaching, our Christian education, our evangelism and mission, and our witness and action for peace and justice.

Runyon then gave three hallmarks for such an *orthopathic* theology. First, Wesley's "bookends" of *creation* and *kingdom,* the fundamental conviction that all creation is to be redeemed by Christ. The world and everything in it is to be brought under the Lordship of Christ—not destroyed, but redeemed.

The second hallmark of *orthopathy* is realism about the present order of things. "We are a part of a world that has corrupted God's good creation and become insensitive and deaf to God's will and way." The gospel forces us to see the alienation and estrangement of the present order and present the gospel necessity of being reborn into a new order.

Thus, the final hallmark of *orthopathic theology* is the familiar word of John 3:7: "You must be born from above."

Runyon's insight helps us think clearly about how we provide the opportunities for the "heart strangely warmed" and the structures of care that will be settings for the transformation of our whole life and total experience. When Wesley insisted that "true Christianity cannot exist without the inward experience and the outward practice of justice, mercy, and truth," he brought orthodoxy, orthopraxis, and orthopathy together and gave us our marching orders.

## OUR WORLDWIDE PARISH

There are many marks of United Methodist style. In the next chapter, we will deal with discipline and means of grace, which are a part of our style. For now, let's look at one other distinctive mark.

It is gathered up in Wesley's popular saying, "The world is my parish." That word captures the style of the Methodist movement—a concern for all humankind, a spending of ourselves and our resources that all the world might be brought to Christ.

Now we need to know that Wesley came to this position "kicking and screaming." His decision to join Whitefield in preaching in the fields to the poor and to coal miners was a difficult one. He fought against it. Whitefield was having great success in reaching for Christ those for whom the established church paid no attention. He sent for John Wesley, knowing his preaching power and organizing skill. Up to this point, Wesley had only preached in regular church services while in England. Should he accept Whitefield's appeal and help with the open-air meetings in Bristol? Charles insisted that he not do it. But John practiced what he preached. He called on the Christian fellowship for guidance. He submitted the decision to the Fetter Lane Society, and they decided he should go. Wesley's *Journal* for Saturday, March 31 reads:

> In the evening, I reached Bristol, and met Mr. Whitefield there. I could scarce reconcile myself at first to this strange way of preaching in the fields, of which he set me an example on Sunday; having been all my life (until very lately) so tenacious of every point relating to decency and order, that I should have thought the saving of souls almost a sin if it had not been done in a church."

Wesley spoke to a little society on Sunday evening using the Sermon on the Mount—"one pretty remarkable precedent of field-preaching," he observed, "though I suppose there were churches at that time also." The next day, Monday, Wesley reported in his *Journal:*

> At four in the afternoon I submitted to be more vile, and proclaimed in the highways the glad tidings of salvation, speaking from a little eminence in a ground adjoining the city, to about three thousand people. The scripture on which I spoke was this, . . . "The Spirit of the Lord is upon Me, because He hath anointed Me to preach the gospel to the poor."

Snyder sums up what happened:

> Characteristically, Wesley immediately began to organize. He formed a number of societies and bands and on May 9 acquired a piece of property where he built his "New Room" as a central meeting place. When Whitefield returned to America in August, Wesley was left totally in charge of the growing work. He divided his time between Bristol and London, concentrating on open-air preaching, organizing bands and speaking at night to an increasing number of societies.
>
> The Wesleyan Revival had begun. From the beginning it was a movement largely for and among the poor, those whom "gentlemen" and "ladies" looked on simply as part of the machinery of the new industrial system. The Wesleys preached, the crowds responded and Methodism as a mass movement was born (*The Radical Wesley,* pp. 32-33).

That's what Methodism is all about—a missional and evangelical witness and outreach that sees the world as our parish—and every person in the world, rich and poor, educated and uneducated, without regard to race—every person as a person for whom Christ died.

My friend, George (Chuck) Hunter, has told a thrilling story—one of those lively vignettes of Methodist history that gives us our vision for now and the future.

A great Methodist leader named C. C. McCabe was the leader of new church extension for the Methodist Episcopal Church in about 1881. He was a prodigious planner, strategist, fund-raiser, and mobilizer. Under his leadership for sustained years, the Methodist Episcopal Church averaged starting one new congregation a day, and some months averaged two congregations a day. One particular day he was traveling to help launch a round of new church plantings in Oregon, Idaho, and Washington, when he picked up a newspaper that had recorded the speech delivered in Chicago by Robert G. Ingersoll, a famous philosopher and agnostic, to the annual convention of a group that imagined itself to be the wave of the future, the Free-thinkers Association of America. In this speech, Ingersoll contended that the churches of the United States of America were in a terminal condition and in another generation there would be few, if any, of them left, which, on the whole, would be a good thing. That incensed McCabe. He got off the train at the next town, went to the Western Union office, dictated a telegram, and sent it to Ingersoll at the convention that was still meeting in Chicago. The telegram read, "Dear Bob: In the Methodist Church we are starting more than one new congregation a day, and we propose to make it two. Signed, *C. C. McCabe*. P. S. All hail the power of Jesus' name."

That was the first of many spirited exchanges and debates between them. The word about that telegram got out and there evolved a folk hymn, part of which went like this:

> The infidels, a motley band,
> In counsel met and said,
> The churches are dying across the land,
> And soon, they'll all be dead.
> When suddenly a message came,
> And caught them with dismay,
> Reading, "All hail the power of Jesus' name,
> We're building two a day."

> *Chorus*

> We're building two a day, dear Bob,
> We're building two a day.

> All hail the power of Jesus' name,
> We're building two a day.

(quoted from George G. Hunter III in his address, "The Challenge We Face," *The Advance,* published by The Asbury Theological Seminary, Parthenon Press, Nashville, Tennessee, Vol. 31, No. 4, pp. 9-10).

It *has* happened before. It *can* happen again. It *should* happen. It *will* happen again when we United Methodists recover the warm heart, when we provide structures of love and care, and when we get a passion for ministry and mission, believing "the world is our parish."

## *QUESTIONS FOR PERSONAL REFLECTION*

1. Most of us have been members of more than one congregation. Look back over your experience with different congregations. Which ones have been plagued by xenophobia? What was the primary "group" of persons who were feared or mistrusted?

2. Has the experience of a "catholic spirit" (pages 93-95) been a significant part of your life and involvement in the church? Why? Why not?

3. Where in your life today, and in what aspect of your congregation's life, do you find the experience of the "warm heart" (page 96) strengthened and sustained?

4. In what way(s) is your congregation acting out the affirmation that "the world is our parish" (pages 98-99)?

In what way do you personally participate in the challenge of this claim?

5. Theodore Runyon describes three dimensions of Christian faith and life
   (page 97): *orthodoxy* (right belief), *orthopraxis* (right conduct), and
   *orthopathy* (right desire). Describe something of your own experience of
   these dimensions.

## QUESTIONS FOR GROUPS SHARING

1. Discuss whether your congregation is sick with xenophobia. If it is, what group is it that is feared or mistrusted? Why is this so?

2. Wesley said that a "catholic spirit" is not *speculative latitudinarianism* (pages 94-95). We can translate that to mean that a catholic spirit does not mean "pluralism," or allowing folks to believe whatever they wish to believe. Talk about this in the light of how you perceive and experience modern Methodism.

3. Invite persons to share their experiences of the warm heart in Christian fellowship.

4. What might your group do in your congregation to make it more a fellowship of the warm heart?

5. Have someone read aloud the material from Theodore Runyon on *orthodoxy, orthopraxis,* and *orthopathy.* Begin with the third full paragraph on page 97, and read through to the end of the section on page 98. Discuss the meaning of this material and the challenge it presents for your congregation. How are you providing or failing to provide settings where people can grow in grace and discipleship and where the fruits of the Spirit can be cultivated?

6. Discuss what your congregation is doing to confirm that the world is its parish.

# Chapter IX
# *Discipline and Means of Grace*

*I appeal to you therefore, brothers and sisters, by the mercies of God, to present your bodies as a living sacrifice, holy and acceptable to God, which is your spiritual worship. Do not be conformed to this world, but be transformed by the renewing of your minds, so that you may discern what is the will of God—what is good and acceptable and perfect* (Rom. 12:1, 2).

As United Methodists, we have an equal and zealous emphasis on personal *and* social holiness. Wesley said, "As tenacious of inward holiness as a mystic, of outward holiness as a Pharisee."

Now neither the mystic nor the Pharisee was a model championed by Wesley. Yet at times he came near the edge of mysticism, and certainly a good part of his life would reflect the model of a Pharisee who knew the law impeccably, and sought diligently to keep it.

To put the two together in this fashion, I believe, is one of those flashes of genius that come out now and then in Wesley's writings. "As tenacious of inward holiness as a mystic, of outward holiness as a Pharisee." That's a picture we can live with and build upon. It is a picture to hold in our minds as we think about the place of discipline in the Christian life, and of the means of grace as channels of growth and power.

In her usual disarmingly honest and challenging way, Mother Teresa painted the picture clearly in her confession: "Pray for me that I not loosen my grip on the hands of Jesus even under the guise of ministering to the poor."

Doesn't that say it? Isn't that our primary calling as Christians? Isn't that the only way we will get on in being the disciples Jesus calls us to be—gripping the hands of Jesus with such firmness that we can't help but follow his lead?

Following him in that fashion requires discipline. Also, Christ and the church provide means of grace that assist us in the process, and that's our focus in this chapter: discipline and means of grace.

## DISCIPLINE IS ESSENTIAL

Scripture, especially the New Testament, is replete with calls to a disciplined life. This is the process of sanctification. We may call it spiritual formation. Through spiritual discipline, opening ourselves to the shaping power of the indwelling Christ, we grow into the likeness of Christ. It was one of Wesley's primary concerns and a distinctive emphasis of the early Methodist movement that the mind of Christ grow in us. It is one of the marks of United Methodist style—*deliberately chosen discipline*.

Wesley preached an interesting sermon in 1778 entitled, "The Work of God in North America." In it, he sought to describe the various dispensations of divine providence in the American colonies as far back as 1736. In the sermon, Wesley commented on the preaching of George Whitefield, which was one of the major contributing factors to the First Great Awakening in America. On Whitefield's last journey to America, the evangelist lamented that many had drawn back into perdition. Taking note of that, Wesley sought to account for this "falling away." This was his telling statement:

> And what wonder? For it was a true saying, which was common in the ancient church, "The soul and the body make a man; and the spirit and discipline make him a Christian." But those who were more or less affected by Mr. Whitefield's preaching had no discipline at all. They had no shadow of discipline; nothing of the kind. They were formed into no societies. They had no Christian connection with each other, nor were they ever taught to watch over each other's souls. So that if they fell into lukewarmness, or even into sin, he had none to lift him up. He might fall lower and lower, yea into hell, if he would; for who regarded it? (Sermon, "The Works of God in North America," Jackson, *Works,* 7:411).

There are few more insightful quotations of Wesley than this. It clearly shows his feeling about the necessity for discipline in the Christian life.

Wesley put a great emphasis on proclaiming the gospel, as did Whitefield. He never diminished preaching and teaching the Word. But he insisted upon the discipline of gathering with a class or a band. As the Methodist movement became more established, Wesley noted the deterioration of this discipline, and he warned against it:

> Never omit meeting your Class or Band; never absent yourself from any public meeting. These are the very sinews of our Society; and whatever weakens or tends to weaken our regard for these, or our exactness in attending them, strikes at the very root of our community. . . . The private weekly meetings for prayer, examination, and particular exhortation has been the greatest means of keeping and confirming every blessing that was received by the word preached and diffusing it to others. . . . Without this religious connection and intercourse the most ardent attempts, by mere preaching, have proved no lasting use (Jackson, *Works,* 11:433).

Now there are some warnings to be sounded. We must guard against turning our disciplines into an end. To be disciplined is not the goal; the goal is to stay close to Christ, to keep our lives centered in him. We must guard against falling into a salvation-by-works pattern. Grace and faith are still the key. We are not saved by disciplines; we are saved by grace through faith.

## THE MEANS OF GRACE

This leads to our next concern: the means of grace. Again the key is *God uses, we choose*. If we are to mature into wholeness, "to the measure of the full stature of Christ" (Eph. 4:13), if we are going to "put on all the armor which God provides" (Eph. 6:11, NEV), then we must avail ourselves of the "means of grace" which Christ and the church provide.

*Means of grace* is a phrase used by Christians to describe the channels through which God's grace is conveyed to us. By "means of grace," Wesley meant "outward signs, words or actions, ordained by God, and appointed for this end, to be the ordinary channels whereby he might convey to man, preventing, justifying, or sanctifying grace."

Wesley never limited God's grace to these means, nor should we. God may use myriad ways of bestowing grace upon us. Yet, there are some specific ways that God enables us to grow in grace. In his sermon on "The Means of Grace," Wesley insisted that the means of grace had no power within themselves. They were *means*, and using them did not guarantee growth. Use of them was not to be legalistic and/mechanical, but as an opening of ourselves to God's activity in our lives. Wesley divided these ordinary means of grace into two categories:

*Instituted* means of grace, or works of piety; and
*Prudential* means of grace, or works of mercy.

## WORKS OF PIETY

Look briefly first at the five works of piety, the instituted means of grace.
First, *prayer.* Wesley said,

God commands all who desire to receive any grace to pray. All who desire the grace of God are to wait for it in the way of prayer. This is the express direction of our Lord. In the Sermon on the Mount Jesus puts it in the simplest terms: "Ask, and it shall be given you; seek, and ye shall find; knock, and it shall be opened unto you: for everyone that asketh receiveth; and he that seeketh findeth; and to him that knocketh, it shall be opened" (*Works,* I, 278f: Sermons, I, 255-258).

Second, *scripture*. We've said that Wesley was a "man of one Book." He wanted Methodists to be Bible people. In fact, early Methodists were referred to derisively as "Bible-moths."

Wesley's emphasis upon the primacy of scripture was based on the conviction that through the Bible, God gives, confirms, and increases true wisdom. It is the scripture, which, according to Paul's word to Timothy, is "able to instruct you for salvation through faith in Christ Jesus" (2 Tim. 3:15).

Third, *the Lord's Supper,* Wesley said, "All who desire an increase of the grace of God are to wait for it in partaking of the Lord's Supper. This is the direction of our Lord: 'Do this in remembrance of me'" (Weems, *The Gospel of John Wesley,* p. 26). Paul put it this way: "For as often as you eat this bread and drink the cup, you proclaim the Lord's death until he comes" (1 Cor. 11:26).

Wesley believed that not only is the Lord's Supper a *confirming* experience; it is also a *converting* one. His mother, Susanna, received the gift of assurance at the Lord's table.

The Lord's Supper was ordained by God to be a means of conveying to persons either preventing, justifying, or sanctifying grace, according to their particular needs. The persons for whom it was ordained are all who know and feel that they need the grace of God. No fitness is required by a sense of our state of sinfulness and helplessness (*Works,* I, pp. 279f; *Sermons,* I, pp. 251-255).

A fourth instituted means of grace is *fasting*. Now this is the one most of us know least about from direct experience. "Of all the means of grace," Wesley said, "there is scarcely any concerning which persons have run into greater extremes than that of religious fasting."

Some have exalted this beyond all scripture and reason while others have utterly disregarded it. The truth lies between them both. It is not the end but it is a precious means which God has ordained, and which, properly used, will bring God's blessing. It is certain that our Master did not imagine fasting to be a little thing.

Every time of fasting, either public or private, should be a season of exercising all of those holy affections which are implied in a broken and contrite heart. Let it be a season of devout mourning, of godly sorrow for sin. And with fasting should be joined fervent prayer, pouring out our whole souls before God, confessing our sins, humbling ourselves, laying open before him all our wants, guilt, and helplessness. It is a time for enlarging our prayers on behalf of others (*Works,* V, pp. 345-60).

A final instituted means of grace is the *Christian conference*. This was small-group sharing in which true *koinonia,* Christian fellowship, could take place. We referred to it when we talked about the church as the "dwelling place of the wonder of Christian fellowship." The class meetings and bands of early Methodism were the setting for this.

The importance Wesley placed in this means of grace can be seen in two remarks he made. On occasion, he stated that "preaching like an apostle without joining together those that are awakened and training them up in the ways of God, is only begetting children for the murderer." This was his opinion after a visit of Pembrokeshire where there were no regular societies. His evaluation was that "the consequence is that nine of the ten once-awakened are now faster asleep than ever." He was fully convinced that wherever this dimension of discipleship was lost, Methodism would cease to be a vital movement (*John Wesley's Message for Today,* p. 84).

These are the works of piety, or the instituted means of grace: prayer, scripture, the Lord's Supper, fasting, and Christian conferencing.
Wesley gave instructions as to how these means should be used.

First, always retain a lively sense, that God is above all means. Have a care, therefore, of limiting the Almighty. He does whatsoever and whensoever it pleaseth Him.
Secondly. Before you use any means, let it be deeply impressed on your soul—there is no *power* in this. It is, in itself, a poor, dead, empty thing: separate from God, it is a dry leaf, a shadow. . . . But, because God bids, therefore I do; . . . I wait for His free mercy, whereof cometh my salvation.
Thirdly. In using all means, seek God alone. In and through every outward thing, look singly to the *power* of His Spirit, and the *merits* of His Son (*Fifty-Three Sermons,* "The Means of Grace," pp. 183-184).

## WORKS OF MERCY

Now a word about the prudential means of grace, or works of mercy. Apart from attending upon all the ordinances of God, Wesley listed two: One, doing no harm; two, doing good. Now, isn't that simple? Yet, how profound in implication—doing no harm, and doing good.
It was clearly underscored in Hebrews: "Pursue peace with everyone, and the holiness without which no one will see the Lord. See to it that no one fails to obtain the grace of God; that no root of bitterness springs up and causes trouble, and through it the many become defiled" (Heb. 12:14-15).
Put simply, the truth is this: *To act as a Christian is a means of grace.* Have you ever thought of it that way? Acting as a Christian expresses itself in what we do, and

what we refuse to do. It is true, as the song says, "They will know we are Christians by our love." It is also true that what we refrain from doing may be the needed telling witness of our lives.

Often when Christians think about what they should *refrain* from doing, sins of the flesh come to mind. Refraining from those goes without saying, so let's look at some other areas:

—Your refusal to order your social life around the cocktail circuit may be a telling witness for the Christian faith.
—Refraining from sharing, in even listening, to destructive gossip, and
—Refusing to affirm the racial bigotry of those around us—either may be our act of grace.
—Refusing to treat any person, whether a mate or an employee, as a thing rather than a person—that's a means of grace. Have you ever stopped to consider the harm we do to other people by not valuing them as persons, or by ignoring, shunning, or not giving them our attention—by failing to be present to them?

We could go on. In our everyday life of acting as a Christian, what we do and what we refrain from doing are means of grace.

*There is also a sense in which we act our way into Christlikeness.* I've never seen persons who *studied* their way into Christlikeness. I've never seen persons who *prayed* or *worshiped* their way into Christlikeness. But I've known countless people who have *acted* their way into Christlikeness. The likeness of Christ shines forth from their lives. All of these people pray; some of them are people with a deep prayer life. They study to varying degrees. They worship. But most of all, they are people whose acts of mercy make them "look like" Jesus.

So what we do or refuse to do in obedience to God becomes a channel of God's grace, which transforms us into the likeness of Christ. And likewise, what we do or refrain from doing in obedience to God becomes a channel for the grace of God to others.

Let me tell you about some of this grace being manifested at least indirectly through the congregation I serve in Memphis, Tennessee. The work of the United Methodist Neighborhood Center is a source of hope and life for countless people. What *grace* this work conveys! Our church is now supporting two full-time missionaries to the city, apart from our ongoing support of the Center's work. Our newest staff person is the Reverend Billy Joe Jackson. What a person of God he is! What commitment and what sanctified imagination! He is so excited, and his excitement is contagious. I thrilled as he talked recently about evangelism among the poor black people in the heart of the city.

Billy Joe has said his ministry is primarily twofold—a ministry of *miracles* and a ministry of *mercy*. He didn't know about Wesley's "works of mercy" category as a means of grace, but he was practicing it. He started a study/prayer group with about twenty men, and they are praying for miracles—jobs for those who are unemployed, health for those who are sick, salvation for those who don't yet trust Christ.

And what about works of mercy? He is visiting people in their homes, entering into their lives and sharing God's Word and love. He is also standing with them in their time of need. The day before I last talked with him, he went to court with a man. His very presence caused the public defender assigned to this fellow to become more interested and more responsible. A man was given hope, and one act of mercy on the part of one person caused another to be gracious and caring.

The Director of Neighborhood Centers, Mark Matheny, told me of an event that took place at the Bread of Life weekly luncheon (a weekly food program at the center in which members of our congregation participate) around Christmastime. A twenty-eight-year-old man was in dire need. He had been unemployed for months and couldn't find a job. One of our Sunday school classes had provided a special offering for him as an act of mercy. But the same week a little girl had been stabbed to death in that community. The unemployed man, though his need was desperate, refused his gift and directed it to be given to the mother of the stabbed girl. *Mercy begets mercy.*

There is a sign in Latin over the doorway of a dining room in San Francisco which says "Caritate Dei." This dining room is in St. Anthony's Catholic Church and feeds some 1,000 needy folks each day. I read a story from the newspaper about a fellow, a young mechanic from Chicago, who went to San Francisco for a vacation, got drunk, was rolled, and ended up in jail without a penny. In jail, he learned of St. Anthony's and went there for a meal when he got out, before he headed back to Chicago. A woman began cleaning the adjoining table. "When do we get down on our knees, lady?" the Chicago mechanic called to her.

"You don't here."

He winks, pulls his red beard. "Then, when's the sermon, the lecture, huh?"

"Aren't any," she replies.

"What's the gimmick?" he persists. His smile is hesitant; he looks uncomfortable.

The well-dressed woman brushes her hair back. She points to a Latin inscription over the entrance: "Caritate Dei."

The brash, young traveler squints up at it and slurs the unfamiliar words. "What's it mean, lady?"

"Out of love for God," she says with a smile and moves to clear another table.

That's one way grace comes to us, and the way it comes to others, in *acts of mercy;* and that grace will eventually prevail. That's the style of a United Methodist—disciplined and using all the means of grace that we might hold on to the hands of Christ, and serve others "out of the love of God."

## *QUESTIONS FOR PERSONAL REFLECTION*

1. Wesley described and recommended a number of "instituted means of grace"—prayer, scripture, the Lord's Supper, fasting, and Christian conference (pages 108-110). Describe something of your own practice of each of these.

Which of these means of grace is the most meaningful to you at this time in your life? Why?

In which of them do you most need to grow and to expand your experience?

2. Recall your most meaningful experience of any one of these means of grace. Make some notes about that experience here.

3. Now think for a moment about the "prudential means of grace"—about works of mercy such as avoiding evil and injustice and doing good to others (pages 110-11). We often think of "good works" more as a *result* than as a *means* of grace. In your own experience, how have works of mercy been a means of grace, both for yourself and for others?

4. Who is the most Christlike person you know? Write two or three paragraphs describing that person.

Now think about the person you have described. How do you think he/she became so Christlike?

## QUESTIONS FOR GROUP SHARING

1. Invite persons to share their experiences of the instituted means of grace: Which of the means do they practice? Which do they find most meaningful?

2. Talk about why some of the means are seldom, maybe never, practiced.

3. Discuss how this study group has been a discipline of Christian conferencing.

4. Invite two or three people to describe the most Christlike person they know. After each description, ask the group to name the things that characterize the person. Are there any traits that all of the persons seem to have in common?

5. Discuss the role of the instituted and the prudential means of grace in the Christlike lives of the persons described in the previous question. Are the means of grace obvious or hidden in their lives?

6. Respond to the author's claim (page 111) that, in his experience, most people who are Christlike have *acted* their way into Christlikeness.

7. Spend the balance of your time together talking about any issues that have been raised during the course of this study—especially any issues that call for more discussion or action. Also, consider where your group may go from here. Have you considered seeing this group as an ongoing means of grace in your life together—"going on to salvation"?